A CRITIQUE OF THE PHILOSOPHY OF BEING OF
ALFRED NORTH WHITEHEAD
IN THE LIGHT OF
THOMISTIC PHILOSOPHY

A Critique of the Philosophy of Being of Alfred North Whitehead in the Light of Thomistic Philosophy

A DISSERTATION

Submitted to the School of Philosophy of the Catholic University of America in Partial Fulfillment of the Requirements for the Degree of Doctor of Philosophy

By

REVEREND LEO A. FOLEY, S.M., M.A.

WIPF & STOCK · Eugene, Oregon

Wipf and Stock Publishers
199 W 8th Ave, Suite 3
Eugene, OR 97401

A Critique of the Philosophy of Being of Alfred North Whitehead in the Light of Thomistic Philosophy
A Dissertation
By Foley, Leo A.
ISBN 13: 978-1-4982-9487-4
Publication date 4/18/2016
Previously published by The Catholic University of America Press, 1946

TO MARY IMMACULATE

TABLE OF CONTENTS

	PAGE
PREFACE	ix

PART ONE—EXPOSITION OF WHITEHEAD'S PHILOSOPHY

CHAPTER

I. WHITEHEAD'S PHILOSOPHICAL AIM AND BACKGROUND	1
II. WHITEHEAD'S THEORY OF KNOWLEDGE	12
III. WHITEHEAD'S THEORY OF BEING AND BECOMING	28
IV. WHITEHEAD'S EXPLANATION OF CAUSALITY	41
V. GOD IN WHITEHEAD'S PHILOSOPHY	59

PART TWO—CRITIQUE OF WHITEHEAD'S PHILOSOPHY

FOREWORD	87

CHAPTER

VI. CRITIQUE OF WHITEHEAD'S THEORY OF KNOWLEDGE	90
VII. CRITIQUE OF WHITEHEAD'S THEORY OF BEING AND BECOMING	107
VIII. CRITIQUE OF WHITEHEAD'S PHILOSOPHY OF CAUSE	130
IX. CRITIQUE OF WHITEHEAD'S PHILOSOPHY OF GOD	146
GENERAL CONCLUSION	165
BIBLIOGRAPHY	167

PREFACE

Ideas, good and bad, are productive, and a teacher of ideas can have a vast influence in the propagating of good and bad ideas. We have only to review the influence of German Idealism upon German and English Romanticism to see this realized. Similarly, today, in the United States, we are reaping the fruit, good and bad, of ideas that have been sown during the past several decades. Some of them we accept, some we reject. All of them deserve our investigation, insofar as is within our power to investigate them, in order that, as followers of truth, we may sift the good from the bad. Hence, we must be familiar not only with our own Scholastic philosophy, but also with the philosophies of non-Scholastics. We must know the modern mind by knowing the philosophers who shape the modern mind. We must be prepared to discriminate between the demagogues and the sincere philosophers. We must know in what way the philosophy we accept is superior, not only in the speculative order but also in the practical order, to the non-Scholastic systems. For true practice is the fruit of speculation, not its opponent.

Among the sincere and well known philosophers of our day, an outstanding representative of mathematical neo-realism, is Alfred North Whitehead, Professor Emeritus of Philosophy at Harvard University, whose philosophy we investigate here. Professor Whitehead was born on Feb. 15, 1861, at Ramsgate in the Isle of Thanet, Kent, England. After the usual classical education, he entered Trinity College of Cambridge University in 1880, where, both as an undergraduate and as a fellow (1865) he concentrated almost exclusively on mathematics. Here, also, he wrote extensively on mathematics and symbolic logic. From 1911–1914 he taught at the University College, London, and in 1914 he became a professor at the Imperial College of Science and Technology in Kensington, where he remained for ten years. In 1924 he was invited to join the Faculty of the School of Philosophy of Harvard University, where he taught philosophy and gave visiting lectures. In 1937, at the age of seventy-six, he became Professor Emeritus, and since has lived in retirement.

His early works have been in mathematics, the most important of which are his collaborations with Bertrand Russell in several editions of *Principia Mathematica*. Of his philosophical works, the more important are listed in the bibliography at the end of this work. Of these, by far, the most important is *Process and Reality*, a professed exposition of his philosophy. *Process and Reality* is the fundamental text in any consideration of Whitehead.

Concerning the method used in this investigation, we shall, in the first half of this work and after an exposition of his philosophical aim and background, consider Whitehead's theories of (i) knowledge, (ii) being and becoming, (iii) causality, (iv) God. The second half of the work will be a critique of these subjects from the standpoint of the philosophy of St. Thomas. In the critique, we shall, in the first half of each chapter, consider St. Thomas's treatment of the problem at hand, and then, in the second half, contrast Whitehead's theory with that of St. Thomas. There is a purpose in treating a theory of knowledge before treating the objective metaphysical content of both Whitehead's and St. Thomas's philosophies. Truth is defined as 'adequatio rei et intellectus,' and hence is dipolar, one term of which is reality, the other the human mind. Any philosophy, then, will be dipolar, and any possible weakness in it will be due to the philosopher's approach to reality and his view of the knowableness of reality. Furthermore, a man's approach to reality is going to color his interpretation of reality, at least to a certain extent. Hence, since certain features of Whitehead's interpretation of reality can be explained in view of his mental background, it is appropriate to consider his theory of knowledge in order to see how he approaches an understanding of reality.

In undertaking the above proposed program, the purpose is threefold: (i) to give, as far as possible, an objective statement of Whitehead's philosophy chiefly in his own words; (ii) to offer a critique of that philosophy in the light of Thomistic principles; and (iii) to show that Thomistic principles, profoundly abstract as they are, are very much in touch with reality and are a much more satisfactory interpretation of it.

It would, perhaps, be better if, in the presentation of Whitehead's philosophy, all Thomistic critique could be avoided and kept for the second part. However, for the sake of clarity and to avoid repetition later on in the work, some critical comparisons from the point of view of Thomism will be found in the first part. Needless to say, criticism is not only negative.

Before closing this introduction, I would like to offer my sincere gratitude to the Very Reverend Ignatius Smith, O.P., Dean of the School of Philosophy, not only for his encouraging interest in this work and his careful reading and valuable criticism of this text, but also for his kindly interest for all the work undertaken by the author in the School of Philosophy of the Catholic University of America. I would also like to extend my thanks to the Reverend Doctor Charles A. Hart under whose patient and helpful guidance this study has been undertaken; to the Reverend Doctor Joseph B. McAllister, S.S., for his careful and valuable criticism of the text; to the members of the Faculty of the School of Philosophy for their friendly encouragement; to Miss Margaret Kelly, secretary to the Dean of the School of Philosophy, for the many ways in which she has proved helpful to the author.

Finally, I would like to thank the Very Reverend Nicholas A. Weber, S.M., S.T.D., Provincial of the Washington Province of the Society of Mary, on whose advice I undertook my studies at the Catholic University. To him, as well as to the Very Reverend Anthony Chouinard, S.M., M.A., Superior of the Marist College, Washington, D. C., the Faculty members and scholastics of Marist College, for the kindly interest of all of these Religious confreres, do I wish to express a debt of gratitude.

The Feast of the Annunciation, 1946.

ABBREVIATIONS

Works of Aristotle

Met.—*Metaphysics*
Phys.—*Physics*

Works of St. Thomas

S.T.—*Summa Theologica*
C.G.—*Summa Contra Gentiles*
De Pot.—*De Potentia*
De Spirit. Creat.—*De Spiritualibus Creaturis*
De Verit.—*De Vertitate*
Qq. Dd.—*Quaestiones Disputatae*
In I Sent.—*Commentary on the Sentences of Peter Lombard*
In I Met.—*Commentary on Aristotle's Metaphysics.*

PART ONE

EXPOSITION OF WHITEHEAD'S PHILOSOPHY

CHAPTER I

WHITEHEAD'S PHILOSOPHICAL AIM AND BACKGROUND

The aim of any philosophy is to give the ultimate natural explanation of reality and of every phase of reality. In doing so, it must answer three questions: (i) What are the operations of each and every component of reality? (ii) What constitutes the essence of each and every component of reality as well as all reality itself? (iii) Why is reality what it is and why do things operate as they do? Hence, philosophy, in answering the above questions, must be founded on: (i) the principle of identity; (ii) the principle of non-contradiction; (iii) the principle of sufficient reason.

To fulfill such an aim is a formidable task. Reality is so vast, so complex, that it is physically impossible to do so in detail. Hence, philosophy must be an abstract science, drawing its data primarily from reality, with a certain dependence upon the natural and mathematical sciences, defining and applying ultimate principles that will interpret and explain reality and all its components. Hence, philosophy is defined as 'the science of all reality, through its ultimate principles, by the light of human reason.' A true philosophy will fulfill that definition. If it fails to do so, it is incomplete. A system that sets out to accomplish that aim and fails to do so is inconsistent.

It may readily be seen that a philosophy must be abstract. The formulation of a philosophy is that of intellectual simplification through intellectual insight. It is the abstraction of principles out of a maze of facts. Applied philosophy is the application of those principles to reality, the assigning of a sufficient reason, a sufficient explanation, to the confusion of detail. The knowledge and use of true principles can well be called the norm of the depth of a philosopher. Coherence and consistency in a philosophical system, its agreement with extra-mental reality (which might well be a definition of truth), these are signs of the truth of a philosophy. Hence, as Aristotle says, the wise man (which the philosopher should be) is the man who knows ultimate principles.[1] The

---

[1] *Met.* I, 2; 982a 1.

philosopher, since his is the science of ultimate principles, should be, literally, the 'lover of wisdom.'

Professor Alfred North Whitehead is acclaimed one of the leading philosophers of the Twentieth Century. He has taught philosophy for years. He has written books on it, and has formulated his own philosophy. Insofar as he represents a philosophical movement founded on mathematics, the burden of this work will be the investigation of his philosophy in the light of the Thomistic requirements set down above. Such requisites have been recognized as the norms of philosophy for centuries, almost until the popular repudiation of philosophy by Auguste Compte. The object of this present chapter is to investigate the aim and background of Dr. Whitehead's philosophical system.

The aim and background of Whitehead's philosophy have been here deliberately coupled as the immediate object of this chapter. It is somewhat unfair to judge a philosopher without taking his background into consideration. Every man, is, to a great extent, a man of his-times, and his intellectual background is greatly shaped by his intellectual content of his times. Hence, although we must judge a man's intellectual acumen in view of his true interpretation of reality, we must take into account his intellectual heritage and judge accordingly. Hence we now consider his aim in the light of his background.

Whitehead certainly has a philosophical aim. He defines philosophy as follows:

"Speculative philosophy is the endeavour to frame a coherent, logical, necessary system of general ideas in terms of which every element of our experience can be interpreted."[2]

Explicit in his philosophy is the object of transcending and completing the specialized sciences. As he says:

"Thus the one aim of philosophy is to challenge the half-truths constituting the scientific first principles. The systematization of knowledge cannot be conducted in watertight compartments. All general truths condition each other; and the limits of their application cannot be adequately defined apart from their correlation by yet wider generalities. The criticism of principles must chiefly take the form of determining the proper meanings to be assigned to the fundamental notions of the various

---

[2] *Process and Reality*, p. 2.

sciences, when these notions are considered in respect to their status relatively to each other. The determination of this status requires a generality transcending any special subject-matter."³

Now, what, besides his intellectual acumen, are Dr. Whitehead's qualifications to follow out this aim? What is his intellectual background? He tells us in his own words, in his brief autobiography in Schilpp's anthology *The Philosophy of Alfred North Whitehead*,⁴ that in the many years he spent at Cambridge University (1880-1910) the emphasis was primarily upon mathematics. Coupled with that, in his life as a student and as a fellow, was active participation in an intellectually inclined discussion group. Both of these play an important part in the formulation of his philosophy.

From his mathematical background came, of course, his mathematical approach to reality, and his introduction to the works of Descartes, the German philosophers, especially Leibniz, who had a large influence in the shaping of Whitehead's philosophy. He says that he could never read the works of Hegel, because of some remarks made by the latter on mathematics. This adds a strange note, as we shall see later on in this chapter.

From the discussions with his friends, discussions in the fields of literature and history especially, and from reading sources necessary for those discussions, he gained his acquaintance with such philosophers as Bacon, Locke, Hume, Berkely, each of whom has contributed an influence to Whitehead's philosophy.

We see, then, a highly specialized training in mathematics especially in the fields of algebra, calculus, and symbolic logic, and a student's interest in history, literature, and British and German philosophy. From this background has evolved his philosophy, a mathematical philosophy, a mathematical interpretation of reality. There is one further fact to be noted, namely, that Whitehead, in his teaching career, held a science professorship for ten years before his appointment as Professor of Philosophy at Harvard.

We may say now, what we are to see in the rest of this work, that Whitehead's philosophy is a mathematical philosophy of reality. A mathematical philosophy is a system of thought that attempts to explain reality through abstract mathematical forms

---
³ *Ibid.*, p. 15.
⁴ Schilpp, *The Philosophy of Alfred North Whitehead*, p. 7 ff.

and relations. There is this to be noted in a mathematical philosophy, namely, that whereas metaphysical abstraction is always consonant with reality, since it explains reality through the twofold principles of act and potency (or capacity and actuality), mathematical abstraction is on a tangent to reality, since, although remotely based upon quantity, it is largely a matter of abstract relations between the abstraction of extension, the abstraction of ponderosity and volume, and the abstraction of angles. Monsignor Sheen, in his book *The Philosophy of Science*, gives an excellently illustrative example taken from Eddington's *The Nature of the Physical World*. The phenomenon to be explained is that of an elephant sliding down a slope. The mathematical interpretation is that of the relation of two tons of ponderosity against a sixty degree angle, without reference either to the elephant or to the slope. It is a matter of pointer readings.[5] Similarly, a mathematical philosophy interprets reality in terms of 'parabolae,' 'vector characters,' and 'matrices.'

Since also this interpretation of reality is in terms of abstractions remotely based upon reality, we can see the grounds of mysticism in a mathematical philosophy. By mysticism, of course, we understand the natural mysticism of idealism, not supernatural mysticism in the order of infused knowledge or of Grace. We can also see an analogy to Plato's idealism, due to the analogy between Plato's explanation of reality in terms of activity and ideal forms and the mathematical interpretation in terms of the changing world and the pervading mathematical forms. Moreover, Plato had a great admiration for mathematics. Plato's mathematics was geometry, which, although abstracted from reality, is still in closer union with reality than algebra or calculus, the especially relativistic branches of mathematics. The irony of this position is that algebra was not developed by Platonists, but by Arabian Aristotelians. The Platonic mathematicians who reject Aristotle are in the dubious position of depending upon Aristotelians for their mathematics.

However, because of this analogy between Plato's idealism and the mathematical interpretation of reality, we can see where Whitehead claims to be a follower of Plato. We can also see that

---

[5] Sheen—*Philosophy of Science*, p. 19 ff; a quotation from Eddington's *The Nature of the Physical World;* pp. 251–254.

from the relativism of higher mathematics Whitehead and the other mathematical philosophers tend to be relativists.

So much for Whitehead's *mathematical* background. There is also his acquaintance with the English philosophers Locke, Hume, and Berkely. This has brought him close to *empiricism*, into an investigation of it, some phases of which he has accepted and others he has rejected. Even though his desire is to transcend the limitations of both mathematics and the sciences, his familiarity with science and with the English empiricists and idealists has left its traces in his philosophy. Locke, Hume, Berkely, and Kant have had their greatest influence in his theory of knowledge. As we shall see, he is a champion of the validity of sense knowledge and the causality of the sense object. He is cautious about intellectual knowledge—stating that its purest activity is to be found in pure, abstract mathematics. He tries to save intellectual knowledge by falling back upon intuition and emotions. Concerning intuition he is a great admirer of Bergson and agrees with Bergson's position of the purity of intuition in contrast to the impurity and uncertainty of intellectual knowledge.

These elements have not all and at once entered into Whitehead's philosophy, for his philosophy has passed through its evolution. It began as a theory of mathematics, became more philosophical, and has finally emerged a definite philosophy with a definite dependence upon mathematics.

Now, just what has been the contribution of his background to his philosophy? That is not too easy to determine. Whitehead's view towards other philosophies is that a philosophy is never refuted but only abandoned.[6] Hence, he feels free to agree with certain doctrines and phases of all philosophies (except Scholasticism) and to disagree with other doctrines and phases. He is then, an eclectic. He feels and acknowledges the contributions of many philosophies upon his own and he attempts to transcend and correct them.

It is not easy to determine the individual philosophers who have had the greatest influence upon him. He claims that his philosophy is on the whole Platonic, insofar as it is in keeping with the European tradition, which he characterizes as a "series of footnotes to Plato."[7] After an investigation into Whitehead's philosophy,

---
[6] *Process and Reality*, p. 9.
[7] *Ibid.*, p. 66.

we may conclude that the one who has had the greatest influence upon him is Leibniz. We may conclude that Whitehead's 'philosophy of organism' is Leibniz's monadology brought up to date. Descartes and Spinoza have also had a great influence upon him. In the field of epistemology, he is greatly indebted to Locke and is in almost complete agreement with Bergson.

We must enlarge upon the above somewhat. All of Whitehead's philosophy is centered around the 'actual entity,' which is the fundamental component unit of all reality, and which is the sufficient reason of all reality. Hence, Whitehead terms it "the ultimate matter of fact." The notion of a component unit of reality being its own sufficient reason is taken from Descartes and his notion of 'res verae.' Whitehead acknowledges his dependence upon Descartes, but does not take much else from Descartes' philosophy.[8]

Having made the principle of sufficient reason the actual thing, Whitehead defines it as a 'growing-together.'[9] The principle of sufficient reason, the thing, is actually a unit of change. Everything that exists is a unit of change, and the differentiation of things is through organization. This dynamic monism, based upon units of change and postulating the ultimate to be 'creativity' or process, we can see to be another aspect of Leibniz's monadology. Making the actual entity, the ultimate thing, a unit of change, and postulating a universe composed of these units of change, shows the clear influence of Leibniz, whose monads were units of self-activity. The influence, and almost imitation, of Leibniz's monadology is striking.

In proposing the 'actual entity' Whitehead is advancing a one-substance philosophy. For substance, he has substituted process. The actual entity is a unit of activity, and this activity is a process of self-perfection, which Whitehead calls 'self-causation.' For this notion, he claims a dependence on and an adaptation of Spinoza's notion of a thing's being a 'causa sui.'[10] In so doing, he replaces Spinoza's 'modes of being' with the 'actual occasion.'[11]

The above philosophers are some of those upon whom Whitehead has drawn in the formation of his philosophy of extra-mental

---

[8] *Ibid.*, pp. viii, ix.
[9] *Ibid.*, p. 34.
[10] *Ibid.*, p. 135.
[11] *Ibid.*, p. 10.

reality. His sufficient reason he draws from Descartes. The nature of the actual entity as a 'causa sui' is taken from Spinoza. His 'organic universe' is Leibniz's monadology with some variations. For mathematical and physical confirmation, he is constantly drawing upon the contemporary mathematicians and scientists.

While still keeping to the notion of the philosophy of reality, we must note a peculiar factor mentioned earlier, namely, that Whitehead says he has never been able to read Hegel. That factor is peculiar, since in several respects, Whitehead's philosophy appears closely to resemble Hegel's philosophy.

There is first of all Whitehead's attitude towards philosophies. We have seen that Whitehead claims that past philosophies have never been refuted, only abandoned. In that connection, he has the following to say:

> "A new idea introduces a new alternative; and we are not less indebted to a thinker when we adopt the alternative which he discards."[12]

Now, although that does not contain the contradictory note so characteristic of Hegel's thesis, antithesis, and synthesis, still, it seems to bear close resemblance to Hegel's dialectical method. There is the abandonment of the professed philosophy of a given philosopher, the investigation of the alternative to that professed philosophy (and note the wording: "A new idea introduces a new alternative"—in which there seems to be a necessary connection between the new idea and its alternative), and the synthesis of the new idea with its new alternative.

Secondly, and more important, is the resemblance between Whitehead's theodicy and Hegel's explanation of nature as the development of 'Sein,' 'Wesen,' and 'Begriff' on the part of the Absolute. Briefly, that means God as the Idea and exemplar of all things, God in the world, God with the world in Him. This closely resembles Whitehead's explanation of reality in terms of God's 'primordial nature' (God as an ideal), God's 'consequent nature' (God in the world), and God's 'superjective nature' (the world in God.) The resemblance is accidental—although Whitehead must undoubtedly be acquainted with the main points in Hegel's philosophy—but it is still striking.

Now, what of Whitehead's dependence upon other philosophers

---

[12] *Process and Reality*, p. 16.

in his theory of knowledge? Concerning perception, Whitehead is refreshingly a realist. This is undoubtedly due to his intimate acquaintance with science. He openly admits the causality of extra-mental sense objects in knowledge. Concerning intellectual judgment—what we term 'ratiocination'—he follows Locke almost literally. Our notion of ratiocination is his 'suspended judgment.' Briefly, his position is that the mind can judge concerning facts, but when it comes to what we would call the judgment of propositions, the mind must await further facts until the proposition becomes so patent that the mind must either affirm or deny. Whitehead uses the term 'proposition' but has a different signification of it. It is akin to our notion of the reduction of potency to act. Since the mind cannot rationalize in our sense of the term, save in pure and abstract mathematics, it must fall back upon imagination in generalizations. We must capture our first principles "with a flash of insight" and we must frequently make use of an "imaginary leap."[13] There is mention of "imaginative generalizations," for metaphysical categories are "tentative formulations."[14] With this in mind, we can readily see Whitehead's adoption of intuition (or the 'intuitive judgment') and his agreement with Bergson's pure intuition.

The above is, I believe, enough to give a brief exposition of Whitehead's eclecticism. He selects from Descartes, Spinoza, Leibniz (especially), in the formulation of his theory of reality. He is attempting to give a dynamic interpretation to all of reality. He is following his mathematical and scientific training, and he calls upon authors whose philosophies seem to contribute to his intended philosophy of reality. His philosophy of knowledge is empirical, and here he depends upon Locke. The mystical strain of the mathematical philosopher makes itself felt in intuition, wherein he agrees to a great extent with Bergson.

There remains to list some of the characteristics of Whitehead's philosophy. Of it we may say the following:

1. Its aim is to give a rational explanation of all experience.
2. It is analogical to Platonism, largely due to mathematics.
3. For the same reason, it is relativistic. One of Whitehead's strongest postulates is that nothing has any meaning save in relation.

---
[13] *Process and Reality*, p. 6.
[14] *Ibid.*, p. 7, cf. p. 12.

4. It contains, therein, a great deal of natural mysticism, ending in a naturalistic cosmic theism, a naturalistic account of a naturalistic immortality.

5. It may be summarized as a dynamic monism.

There is one more characteristic not listed above which deserves special mention. This characteristic is Whitehead's peculiar use of terms. He claims that words are inadequate because of their limited and changing meanings. Hence he formulates his own terms, such terms as 'prehensions,' 'concrescences,' 'subject-superject.' That makes his philosophy difficult to read, more difficult to understand.

We may close this chapter with three observations. (i) We may say, on the whole, that Whitehead has formulated a definite system of philosophy based ultimately upon a mathematical interpretation of reality, transcending, at least in intention, the particular sciences. This philosophy is analogical to Platonism insofar as it is the interplay of a world of action and a world of extrinsic forms. It is a dynamic monism characterized by relativism and natural mysticism. (ii) Although various phases of Whitehead's philosophy strike us as inconsistent, out of touch with reality, and to a certain extent superficial, we must still give Whitehead credit as a deep and earnest thinker. (iii) We must, in all fairness, respect, and courtesy, judge these inconsistencies in the light of Whitehead's philosophical background. It is true that the ultimate criterion of a philosophy is its understanding, explanation, and presentation of truth. Yet, we must realize that a man approaches truth from the point of view of his own intellectual background. What a man does with his materials is also a measure of a man's mental acumen. If Whitehead's background is, on the one hand mathematical and on the other hand empirical, we must keep that background in mind in seeing if and how he attains the end he has set before him, namely, to give a complete and general explanation of every item of experience.

fundamental tenets in Whitehead's theory of knowledge. As we know, a theory of knowledge is an instrument in the founding of a philosophy. Whitehead is attempting to found a philosophy, which philosophy is:

> ". . . the endeavor to frame a coherent, logical, necessary system of general ideas in terms of which every element of our experience can be interpreted."[2]

That, of course, is laudable. Knowledge begins with experience, our own experience and the experience of others. It is not limited to experience, however. We also know certain basically metaphysical truths, truths of all reality, axioms, and we build a system that explains all reality, not merely our own experience. Does Whitehead have anything to say about basic metaphysical principles? He does.

> "Metaphysics is nothing but the description of generalities which apply to all the details of practice.
> "No metaphysical system can hope entirely to satisfy these pragmatic tests. At the best such a system will remain only an approximation to the general truths which are sought. In particular, there are no precisely stated axiomatic certainties from which to start. There is not even the language in which to frame them."[3]

Those words were written about the year 1928. The following words were written about 1941, and delivered in a lecture at Harvard University on April 22, 1941. They are the concluding words of a lecture entitled *Immortality*.

> "My point is that the final outlook of Philosophic thought cannot be based upon the exact statements which form the basis of special sciences.
> "The exactness is a fake."[4]

There is a great deal of empiricism in those statements, yet there is withdrawal from the empirical sciences. There are no axioms on which to found philosophy, yet there is philosophy. We cannot trust exact statements, yet how can we philosophize with any degree of certainty? Whitehead will answer by saying that we can affirm or deny fact, but when it comes to speculating about reality, we must suspend our judgments, or judge tentatively until facts impress themselves upon our experience. By what means,

---

[2] *Process and Reality*, p. 4.
[3] *Ibid.*, p. 19.
[4] *Immortality*—in the anthology, *The Philosophy of Afred North Whitehead*, p. 700.

then, can we philosophize? We perceive and think by immediate intuition of the world through feelings. The universe is dipolar. Every entity in the world is in immediate union with the adjacent universe. Its end is to be in immediate union with the entire universe. The same is true for our minds. It is in immediate contact, through feelings, with the adjacent world, and potentially with the entire universe. Save for speculation in pure mathematics, there is no thinking independent of the extra-mental world. In order to explain our thinking and perceiving, we have to explain the entire cosmos. There is no independence in Whitehead's universe, for we, as thinking entities, are dependent parts of an organic universe. Just as every other entity in the world is in union with the world through its 'feelings', so we, in our thinking (as well as our other processes) are in immediate union with the entire universe. We are high-grade societies whose union with the world is through our 'thought-feelings.' Our mind is our thinking. We are thinking substances. Here we see the influence of Hume the skeptic and Descartes the idealist upon Whitehead's philosophy, of which, his theory of knowledge is only a phase, a mode, rather than a distinct part.

There is much emotionalism in Whitehead's intuition. That is the common concept of intuition. If we cannot *know* the answer, we *feel* a preference to a certain possible solution. Now, an empiricist, one who rejects metaphysical foundations of knowledge, cannot (if he is consistent with himself) *know* the answers. Hence, he must *feel* the answers. And in Whitehead's philosophy, feelings, among rational entities, are emotional. Whereas in low-grade entities, feelings are natural tendencies, in high-grade entities, feelings are emotions. Hence, our feelings about things known give greater satisfaction to the knowing entity that cold intellectual knowledge would give.

On the satisfaction given the knowing subject by feelings, Whitehead has the following to say.

> ". . . the main function of intellectual feelings is neither belief nor disbelief, nor even suspension of judgment. The main function of these feelings is to heighten the emotional intensity accompanying the valuations in the conceptual feelings involved, and in the more physical purposes which are more primitive than any intellectual feelings."[5]

---

[5] *Process and Reality*, p. 416.

That citation is taken from *Process and Reality*. In *Adventures of Ideas*, Whitehead has much the same to say.

> "I contend that the notion of mere knowledge is a high abstraction, and that conscious discrimination itself is a variable factor only present in the more elaborate examples of occasions of experience. The basis of experience is emotional. Stated more generally, the basic fact is the rise of an affective tone originating from things whose relevance is given."[6]

We might summarize that this way: (i) we can only know facts (empiricism.) (ii) But in order to know facts properly, we must know them in relation to the rest of the world, which is beyond our knowledge. Hence (iii) we must feel the answers, by feeling the fact's relevance to ourselves and to the rest of the world. Intellectual knowledge (save in the realm of higher mathematics) is impure. Intuition through feelings and emotions is the pure and safe knowledge. Whitehead differs somewhat from Bergson's mystic intuition. In this, however, he is one with him. As he says:

> "The stage of existence in which propositional feelings are important, apart from the intellectual feelings, may be identified with Bergson's stage of pure and instinctive intuition."[7]

Hence, by way of concluding these presuppositions, these key postulations to Whitehead's theory of knowledge, we can say, by way of summary:

1. There are no metaphysical axioms on which to base our understanding of reality.

2. Our mind is in union with the entire world through our feelings, and the emotional satisfaction gained through our mental feelings is our guarantee of our mental one-ness with the extramental world.

3. Outside of the realm of higher mathematics, our intellectual feelings are definitely subordinated to our 'propositional feelings' (our feelings of assent or negation). These propositional feelings are identical with Bergson's intuition.

With that background, let us now turn to an investigation of (i) Whitehead's theory of intuitive perception, and (ii) judgment. In this we must remember that his theory of knowledge is going to influence and be influenced by his philosophy of being.

---

[6] *Adventures of Ideas*, pp. 225, 226.
[7] *Process and Reality*, p. 428.

INTUITIVE PERCEPTION

In *Adventures of Ideas*, Whitehead summarizes his theory of sense perception. He speaks about "the old advice that the doctrines which best repay critical examination are those which for the longest period have remained unquestioned."

"The particular agelong group of doctrines which I have in mind is: (1) that all perception is by the mediation of our bodily sense organs, such as eyes, palates, noses, ears, and the diffused bodily organization furnishing touches, aches, and other bodily sensations; (2) that all percepta are bare sensa, in patterned connections, given in the immediate present; (3) that our experience of a social world is an interpretative reaction wholly derivitive from this perception; (4) that our emotional and purposive experience is a reflective reaction derived from the original perception, and intertwined with the interpretative reaction and partly shaping it. Thus the two reactions are different aspects of one process, involving interpretative, emotional, and purposive factors."[8]

We may summarize this by saying that we perceive objects. We perceive them as apart from ourselves in a patterned arrangement, i.e., in some sort of order. Our interpretation is a reaction resulting from this perception. We have an emotional interpretation which helps to shape this primary interpretation and re-interpret it to a certain extent. The interplay of our primary (almost automatic) interpretation and of the emotional interpretation is the process of knowledge, wherein we preceive and understand. We can say that by our primary interpretation we perceive and notice. By our emotional interpretation we understand. In this, we can see intuition and lyricism. We can see that in the process of becoming there is no place for intellectual, Aristotelian categories.

To seek a fuller explanation of this process, we must investigate Whitehead's book *Symbolism, Its Understanding and Effect*, wherein it is explained, and in this we will investigate 'presentational immediacy,' 'objectification,' and 'causal efficacy,' which are the applications of what we have seen above. 'Presentational immediacy' is the awareness of the object perceived by the senses. 'Objectification' we shall see to be something of an approach to sensitive abstraction. 'Causal Efficacy' is our "emotional and purposive experience . . . a reflective reaction derived from the

---

[8] Whitehead, *Adventures of Ideas*, p. 228.

original perception, and intertwined with the interpretative reaction and partly shaping it."⁹

We might note here that Whitehead summarizes the knowing process in what he terms 'symbolism.' All knowledge is symbolism. Our ideas are symbols of things existing outside of us. We express our ideas in symbols, whether they be words or monuments. Although Whitehead's principles deny representative knowledge, he implies it in his theory of symbols.

> The first term to be investigated is 'presentational immediacy.'
> "By 'presentational immediacy' I mean what is usually termed 'sense-perception.' But I am using the former term under limitations and extensions which are foreign to the common use of the latter term.
> "Presentational immediacy is our immediate perception of the contemporary external world, appearing as an element constitutive of our own experience. In this appearance the world discloses itself to be a community of actual things, which are actual in the same sense as we are."¹⁰

Presentational immediacy is the awareness of our environment, and is brought about by the activity of the outside world upon our senses. It is effected through the mediation of the senses, for in high-grade occasions the senses are the channels through which we apprehend our environment. Thus, the wall reflects light of a certain color, which strikes the eye and causes our recognition of that certain color. The quality of the proper object of the sense—for example, color for the eye—is, according to Whitehead, both our sensation and the quality of the thing we perceive, and thus is the relation between the perceiving subject and the thing perceived.¹¹ Furthermore, we perceive spatial relations by reason of sense data.

> "In this appearance, the world discloses itself to be a community of actual things which are actual in the same sense that we are."¹²

The main factors of presentational immediacy are:

> "(1) That the sense-data involved depend on the percipient organism and its spatial relations to the perceived

---
⁹ *Ibid.*, p. 228.
¹⁰ *Symbolism*, p. 21.
¹¹ *Ibid.*, p. 22.
¹² *Ibid.*, p. 21.

organisms; (2) that the contemporary world is exhibited as extended and as a plenum of organisms; (3) that presentational immediacy is an important factor in the experience of only a few high-grade organisms, and that for the others it is embryonic or entirely negligible."[13]

Hence, outside of disclosing the world in its spatial character and disclosing things as being in space, presentational immediacy is barren, although Whitehead calls it "vivid, precise."[14] We shall return to this when we come to 'causal efficacy' and 'symbolic reference.'

The second notion to be considered, and closely associated with presentational immediacy, is 'objectification.' This is the process whereby things outside of us become objectively present within us while still existing formally in themselves outside of us.

"In this explanation of Presentational Immediacy, I am conforming to the distiction according to which actual things are *objectively* in our experience and *formally* existing in their own completeness. I maintain that presentational immediacy is that peculiar way in which contemporary things are 'objectively' in our experience, and that among the abstract entities which constitute factors in the mode of introduction are those abstractions usually called sense-data:—for example, colors, sounds, tastes, touches, and bodily feelings.

"Thus 'objectification' itself is abstraction; since no actual thing is 'objectified' in its 'formal' completeness. Abstraction expresses nature's mode of interaction and is not merely mental."[15]

We must note here Whitehead's different use of terms. We usually consider objective as being outside of the mind. It is thus opposed to 'subjective' which is in the ego. For Whitehead, 'objective' means being in the mind, but not identified with the ego. It is thus opposed by a thing existing 'formally.' Thus, if we have the notion of a chair in our consciousness, the chair has somehow entered into us. Yet it still remains in itself outside of us. In Whitehead's theory, the chair exists 'objectively' in our minds, while it exists 'formally' outside of our minds. The process whereby it becomes a notion in our minds is 'objectification'—

---

[13] *Symbolism*, p. 23.
[14] *Ibid.*, p. 23.
[15] *Ibid.*, p. 25.

namely, making the formal chair 'objective' in our minds, which 'objectification' is abstraction, the causality of our knowledge by the external object.

Unfortunately, Whitehead's peculiar use of technical terms is somewhat confusing at first sight. He uses a time-honored term like 'abstraction,' in a sense that most Scholastic philosophers use it. But then he extends it to mean any interaction between actual occasions. "Abstraction expresses nature's mode of interaction and is not merely mental."[16] This is important. It reflects his philosophy, which implies a dynamic monism of interaction of actual occasions—non-mental with non-mental, mental with non-mental, mental with mental.

> "The conception of the world here adopted is that of functional activity. By this I mean that every actual thing is something by reason of its activity; whereby its nature consists in its relevance to other things, and its individuality consists in its synthesis of other things so far as they are relevant to it."[17]

More than that, this notion of 'objectification'—or interplay of actual occasions—this distortion of abstraction, is the key to Whitehead's metaphysics. In this he is consistent, for he says:

> "This lecture has maintained the doctrine of a direct experience of an external world. It is impossible fully to argue this thesis without getting too far from my topic. I need only refer you to the first portion of Santayana's recent book *Scepticism and Animal Faith*, for a conclusive proof of the futile 'solipsism of the present moment'—or, in other words, utter scepticism—which results from a denial of this assumption. My second thesis, for which I cannot claim Santayana's authority, is that, if you consistently maintain such direct individual experience, you will be driven in your philosophical construction to a conception of the world as an interplay of functional activity whereby each concrete individual thing arises from its determinate relativity to the settled world of other concrete individuals, at least so far as the world is past and settled."[18]

Thus far we have been speaking of the two modes of direct intuition of sense data. The enrichment of this sense data is by

---

[16] *Symbolism*, p. 26.
[17] *Ibid.*, p. 26.
[18] *Symbolism*, p. 28.

'casual efficacy.' This must be treated together with 'symbolic reference,' which symbolic reference is the interplay of presentational immediacy with causal efficacy in the process of knowledge. The necessity for these two is that presentational immediacy is only a cross section of the present, and has no reference to past or future. Hence it is here and gone immediately.

> "The pure mode of presentational immediacy gives no information as to the past or future. It merely presents an illustrated portion of the presented duration. It thereby defines a cross-section of the universe: but does not in itself define on which side lies the past, and on which side the future. In order to solve such questions we now come to the interplay of between the two pure modes. This mixed mode of perception is here named 'symbolic reference.' The failure to lay due emphasis on symbolic reference is one of the reasons for metaphysical difficulties; it has reduced the notion of 'meaning' to a mystery."[19]

Hence, for this relation, for the clarification of our perception as to past and future, we must postulate 'causal efficacy.' Causal efficacy is, we are told:

> ". . . the hand of the settled past in the formation of the present."[20]

Causal efficacy has two important functions: clarification by localization, and the pointing out of the cause of the perception. It is causal efficacy that makes us realize that we see with the eye, hear with the ears, taste with the tongue, etc. That is of minor importance. Of far greater importance is the fact that through causal efficacy we know that the cause of our impressions, or notions, is from the outside. In this stand, Whitehead is consistant with the philosophy of organism and flatly against Hume.

> "These primitive emotions are accompanied by the clearest recognition of other actual things reacting upon ourselves. The vulgar obviousness of such recognition is equal to the vulgar obviousness produced by the functioning of any one of our five senses. When we hate, it is a man that we hate and not a collection of sense-data—a causal, efficacious man."[21]

---

[19] *Process and Reality*, p. 255.
[20] *Symbolism*, p. 50.
[21] *Ibid.*, p. 45.

In *Process and Reality* (pp. 264-266) Whitehead writes expressly against Hume's 'habit of thought' in the example of the man blinking after a bright light is lit. As Whitehead holds, much as Hume may hedge about, the fact still remains that the man will claim that the light made him blink.

Thus, then, it is causal efficacy that adds depth to our perception. It gives the notion of past and future to what is merely a cross-section of the present, presentational immediacy. It is the past acting causally upon the present. Whitehead is emphatic about the past acting upon the present, and maintains that the sense of continuity is the consciousness of the immediate past always lasting over to the present.

We can conclude about causal efficacy in the following words:

"The bonds of causal efficacy arise from without us. They disclose the character of the world from which we issue, an inescapable condition round which we shape ourselves. The bonds of presentational immediacy arise from within us, and are subject to intensifications and inhibitions and diversions according as we accept their challenge or reject it. The sense-data are not properly to be termed 'mere impressions'—except so far as any technical term will do. They also represent the conditions arising out of the active perceptive functioning as conditioned by our own natures. But our natures must conform to the causal efficacy. Thus the causal efficacy *from* the past is at least one factor giving our presentational immediacy *in* the present. The *how* of our present experience must conform to the *what* of the past in us.

"Our experience arises out of the past: it enriches with emotion and purpose its presentation of the contemporary world; and it bequeaths its character to the future, in the guise of an effective element forever adding to, or subtracting from, the richness of the world. For good or for evil,

'Pereunt et Imputantur'."[22]

WHITEHEAD AND SPECULATIVE KNOWLEDGE

What we have seen thus far in this chapter is mostly what the Scholastic philosopher would consider sense perception. Whitehead desires to champion speculative knowledge. His whole philosophy is a speculative system, and one of the ends of his work *Process and Reality* is to repudiate "... The distrust of speculative philos-

---

[22] *Symbolism*, p. 58.

ophy."[23] Yet, when Whitehead tries to explain the processes involved in intellectual knowledge, he writes mystifyingly. His whole theory seems to be a sublimated empiricism in keeping with all the principles of the philosophy of organism. His whole doctrine of 'feelings' is reiterated, but on a higher plane. He explains his theory of intellection in two chapter of *Process and Reality*, namely, *Symbolic Reference*, and *Higher Phases of Experience*. The former treats of what we would call abstract ideas and terms. The latter considers what we call judgments. Both are a matter of our offering (assenting) or rejecting (dissenting) feelings to data that offers itself to the mind.

Whitehead has the mathematician's appreciation of symbols, and keeps that notion of symbols throughout his consideration. In one of his latest writings, an opusculum entitled *Mathematics and the Good*[24] which is incorporated in Schilpp's anthology *The Philosophy of Alfred North Whitehead*, he shows how the algebraic symbols x and y have their meaning only insofar as they can represent now this and now that. They are feelings which we apply to the 'givenness' of any occasion which offers its feelings to our feelings. It is all a matter of feelings, for any perception, whether the simplest forms of sense knowledge or the highest phases of intellectual appreciation are prehensions, that is, the mutual acceptance of feelings, for:

". . . the philosophy of organism attributes 'feeling' throughout the actual world."[25]

Symbols themselves have the element of timelessness about them. They refer to the past, present, or future. They are necessary as a continuity of knowledge, for as we saw, mere 'presentational immediacy' is barren and ephemeral. What is constantly changing in the actual world becomes permanent in our mental feelings.

The application of symbols to reality ('symbolic reference') partakes distinctly of 'presentational immediacy' but only confusedly of 'causal efficacy.'[26] That is why it appears closer to what we would call 'simple apprehension' than to judgment. It is the application of a term or a sign to some datum here and

---

[23] *Process and Reality*, p. viii.
[24] *The Philosophy of Alfred North Whithead*, pp. 666 ff.
[25] *Process and Reality*, p. 268.
[26] *Ibid.*, p. 256.

now offering itself to the mental feelings. Yet it is the presentation of a past truth to a present fact and potentially to a future fact. It is recognition, rather than judgment. Hence it has more to do with immediate inference than with ratiocination.

Ratiocination comes under judgment. Whitehead uses the term 'judgment,' postulates several kinds of judgments, but once again explains them all in terms of feelings. The feelings are affirmative ('adversion') or negative ('aversion'). Each judgment is a proposition, but a proposition of feelings, or rather, the adversion or aversion between feelings.

> "A feeling is termed a 'belief' or is said to include an element of 'belief', when its datum is a proposition, and its subjective form includes, as the defining element in its emotional pattern a certain form, or eternal object, associated with some gradation of character. This eternal object is 'belief-character.'"[27]

Judgment itself is based upon what Whitehead calls 'conscious perception', which is defined as follows:

> "Conscious perception is the feeling of what is relevant to immediate fact in contrast with its potential irrelevance."[28]

In other words, it is the examination of the relevance or irrelevance of an idea (which Whitehead calls a feeling) to a situation, whether the situation be mental or objective. That, we may note, comes very close to William James, for whose psychology Whitehead has high admiration. A judgment has reference to three species among comparative feelings, which three species are: affirmative, negative, or neither.

> "The three species are composed of (i) those feelings in the 'yes-form,' (ii) those feelings in the 'no-form,' and (iii) those feelings in the 'suspense-form.'"[29]

Judgments are twofold: 'intuitive judgments' and 'inferential judgments.' 'Intuitive judgments' are the perception of agreement, disagreement, or suspension of judgment between intellectual feelings and actual entities. Whitehead gives a very complicated explanation of the process involved, and includes the element of imaginative richness. All perception—or judgment—(he uses the two terms interchangeably) is according to patterns. It is a

---
[27] *Process and Reality*, p. 408.
[28] *Ibid.*, p. 409.
[29] *Ibid.*, p. 412.

complicated process whereby we immediately agree, disagree, or suspend our judgment about some actual entities which present their feelings to the intellectual feelings. The element of 'imaginative feelings' and 'propositional feelings' enter in as categories of mental procedure to aid the process, together with 'physical recollection,' 'indicative feeling,' 'predicative feeling.' However, we must remember that the basic process is between 'intellectual feelings' offering themselves either positively, negatively, or suspensively to the offered feelings of actual entities. The other complications are categories of mental processes that enter into the process to aid it.

Concerning 'suspended' judgment, Whitehead follows Locke and apparently accepts all that Locke has to say on judgments. This, of course, is parallel to our notion of mediate judgments.

"Locke's section (IV, XIV, 4), on this subject is short enough to be quoted in full: '*Judgment is the presuming things to be so without perceiving* it . . . Thus the mind has two faculties conversant about truth and falsehood.
'*First.* Knowledge, whereby it certainly perceives, and is undoubtedly satisfied of the agreement or disagreement of any ideas.
'*Secondly.* Judgment, which is the putting ideas together, or separating them from one another in the mind, when their certain agreement or disagreement is not perceived, but presumed to be so; which is, as the word imports, taken to be so before it certainly appears. And if it so unites or separates them as in reality things are, it is right judgment.' "[30]

Notice that this is more a method of uncertainty than of certitude. The judgment is made *before* the truth of the proposition is known. Hence if the thinker is honest, although he makes this so-called judgment, he must suspend this judgment, or rather, hold in suspense his already made judgment, until the certainty of the facts or proposition is known. Hence, Whitehead calls this a 'suspended judgment.'

According to Whitehead, this is between three terms: the 'intellectual feeling,' the relation between the 'objectifying predicate, and 'the imagined practice' in such a way "as to preclude either case of direct judgment."[31] Together with it, again as

---
[30] *Process and Reality*, p. 418.
[31] *Ibid.*, p. 418.

categories of mental processes, are 'physical recollection,' 'indicative feelings,' 'conceptual imagination,' and 'propositional imagination.'

All this explanation of 'intuitive judgments' and 'suspended judgments' seems a highly complicated way of explaining the immediate acceptance of facts or the tentative acceptance of theories. Yet, to be consistent with the whole philosophy of organism, which is a series of 'prehensions' between actual entities, whether these are extra-mental, intra-mental, or between mental and extra-mental actual entities according to the feelings that they mutually offer or repulse, the theory must be as complicated as the entire process between these entities.

Another thing we must note in this theory is that although it is Whitehead's explanation for speculative knowledge, it is thoroughly empirical in its method. It is a complicated explanation of the foundation of empirical epistemology, namely, that we can immediately affirm or deny facts, but that we must suspend judgment or else judge tentatively concerning theories until further facts are ascertained. The element of 'feelings' is Whitehead's contribution to it, in an attempt to combine the scientific empiricism of the descendents (philosophical) of John Locke with the lyrical intuition of Henri Bergson. Bergson had said that intellection was poor in comparison to intuition. Certainly Whitehead makes his 'suspended judgment' far more complex than his already complicated 'intuitive judgment.'

Certainly, intellection, as we know it as a rational process, is missing. Substituted for it is an emotional process, for if 'feelings' do not have direct reference to emotions, than we must ask ourselves just what Whitehead means by words at all. Certainly missing is the traditional notion of 'abstraction,' namely, a process of revealing the necessary element within the known object. Again, certainly missing in it is the traditional notion of the affirmation or negation of two or more ideas already existing in the mind and representative of two objects outside the mind. Instead, there is postulated a complicated system of acceptance or repulsion of 'propositional feelings' in the components of the proposition and the 'intellectual feelings' in the mental equipment of the judging subject. All this is far afield from the traditional notion of abstraction and judging. It is a certainly complicated explanation for something which human nature would consider relatively simple.

SUMMARY

Whitehead's theory of knowledge contains a twofold aspect: his theory of perception and his theory of intellectual activity, or speculative knowledge. Although he claims to be a champion of speculative knowledge, and does formulate a speculative system of philosophy, his method is empirical. It is all explained in terms of organic philosophy.

I. HIS THEORY OF PERCEPTION.
  1. As a part of the vast organic interplay of actual occasions, objects existing outside of the mind enter into the mind, through a mutual offering and acceptance of 'feelings,' and there exist as notions. The manner of doing this is 'objectification' or 'abstraction.'
  2. Thus, we have contact with the outside world through the 'feelings' of sense-knowledge. This is through:
     (a) Presentational immediacy—which is what we ordinarily call sense knowledge, and which is a perceived cross-section of the outside world, existing as a plenum of actual occasions. Presentational immediacy has no reference to past or future.
     (b) Causal efficacy—is the enrichment of sense data in the light of and with the wealth of past experience. It localizes our intuition, and shows knowledge to be the effect of the object acting upon the senses. Thus, it gives perspective to our apprehension.
  3. The knowing process is the interplay of presentational immediacy and casual efficacy, whereby depth is added to our sense perception and proper interpretation is given.

II. HIS THEORY OF SPECULATIVE KNOWLEDGE.
  1. Intuitive judgments are the direct affirmation or negation of facts through the mutual offering and acceptance of 'intellectual feelings' and the 'feelings' of existing actual beings.
  2. Suspended judgments are the mutual offering and acceptance of the 'intellectual feelings' on the one hand, and 'propositional feelings' of the members of the proposition to be considered. The judgment is made tentatively until further facts are known.

This explanation, although it claims to be according to the intuition of Bergson, is more a complicated formulation of the basic facts of empiricism.

CHAPTER III

Whitehead's Theory of Being and Becoming

As a preface to this chapter, we might note that as far as we know, the first major work written by St. Thomas Aquinas, the greatest of Scholastic philosophers, was *De Ente et Essentia*. The first major work of Alfred North Whitehead, written in collaboration with Bertrand Russell, was *Principia Mathematica*. That contrast between St. Thomas and Dr. Whitehead is not for the purpose of trying to compare the two. It is for the purpose of indicating the two approaches to objective reality, the approach of Thomism, which attempted to reach the very being of each and every thing, and a modern approach which tries to explain everything in terms of mathematical concepts. Whitehead, able mathematician that he is, follows the mathematical approach.

As long as man has lived, he has been struck by two obvious observations, namely, that things are and that things change. About him he perceives a continuous change. In the ebb and flow of reality he sees night give way to day, the seasons give way one to the other. He notices that things appear, remain for awhile, and then disappear. He knows that he is constantly growing older, changing in so many ways. In other words, he perceives the obviousness of change.

On the other hand, he also notices a definite stability in all reality. He writes poetry about the 'everlasting hills.' He uses a universal simile or metaphor when he sings *Rock of Ages*. He knows that even though he grow old, he still remains a man in his nature. He observes the orderliness and unchanging constancy in the manner in which night gives way to day. He bases the sciences of meteorology and astronomy on the changes of the seasons and the invariable manner in which the heavenly bodies move or appear to move. Again, in other words, he perceives the obviousness of being. In fine, he notices the essential relation between being and becoming.

There are many sciences which attempt to explain being and becoming. The physicists tries to understand the energy of reality. The mathematician studies the extension of reality. The biologist tries to explain life, while the chemist investigates the internal structure and internal change of all bodies.

Yet there is a science that tries to explain being and becoming as such, that goes far deeper than the particular sciences in an attempt to arrive at the basic principle of all, that investigates the nature of Being, the nature of Becoming. That science is metaphysics, the ultimate natural explanation of being itself. Since metaphysics strives to get at the very being of things, it stands to reason that any philosophy should be primarily metaphysical. If philosophy is a science to explain all things through their ultimate principles by the light of reason, it must necessarily be centered about metaphysics, since no explanation is complete without an attempt to explain the fundamental principle of all reality, being.

With this in mind, we can now investigate the metaphysical content of Whitehead's philosophy. Whitehead claims his philosophy to be a metaphysics. His object is to formulate general principles that adequately explain every item of experience.[1] It is true that he states that first principles cannot be known certainly, rather that "... there are no precisely stated axiomatic certainties from which to start. There is not even the language in which to frame them."[2] This, of course, weakens his philosophy immediately, for, as we shall see, he formulates principles, and then has to force them to fit the basic principles of experience, those basic recognitions of sound principles which are the basis of all sound reasoning.

We find the key to the investigation of his metaphysics in his listing of the categories, which are, as it were, a digest of the philosophy he is to propose. In his 'categorial scheme,' Whitehead advances four classes of categories: The Category of the Ultimate; The Categories of Existence; The Categories of Explanation; and The Categorial Obligations.[3] In these four classes of categories, particularly in the two former, the Category of the Ultimate and the Categories of Existence, we find the principles wherein he advances the existential principles upon which his entire philosophy is founded. The explanation and interrelation of these principles are summarized in the two latter categories, namely, the Categories of Explanation and the Categorial Obligations. His ontological

---

[1] *Process and Reality*, p. 4.
[2] *Ibid.*, p. 18.
[3] *Ibid.*, p. 30 ff.

principles are formulated into a system founded upon four pillars. (There are other principles, but these four are the most important.) These are: 'Dipolarity,' 'The Ontological Principle,' 'the Principle of Relativity,' and 'the Principle of Process.' For a proper understanding of Whitehead's pilosophy, we must have a firm grasp upon these four fundamental principles.

Dipolarity[4] may be said to be 'an actual thing's perception of its relations with that part of the objective universe with which it is in contact.' On the one hand, as one pole of the relation, we have the perceiving subject. On the other, as the opposite pole of the relation, is that which is perceived, namely, the thing's relations with that part of the extra-mental universe with which the entity is in contact. Important to note is that every actual entity in Whitehead's universe, in similarity to the monads in Leibniz's universe, is able to perceive. This is because Whitehead, rejecting what he calls 'two-substance ontology'[5] and with the intention of formulating a 'one-substance cosmology,' tries to use Locke to steer the middle course between the extreme dualism of Descartes and the mental monism of Leibniz. He obviously leans towards Leibniz, and his aim to present a 'one-substance cosmology' is obviously monistic. Yet, he wises to avoid the position of Leibniz, whose monadology makes each thing a self-perceptive activity, and the position of the German idealists, who would make mind the creator of matter. Whitehead realizes that the objective world exists physically and not merely mentally. Hence, he projects Locke's account of mental substance into the essence of each and every existing entity. The result is the dipolarity defined above. Since Whitehead holds that every entity is in some degree perceptive, we may note that his doctrine of the organic universe' is hylozooism in modern garb.

The Ontological Principle may be formulated as follows: 'The ultimate reason of any existing entity is to be found in the ultimate existing component unit of the universe, the actual entity.' More briefly, 'The sufficient reason of anything is to be found in the actual entity.' We may quote Whitehead's wording of that principle:

"That every condition to which the process of becoming

---

[4] *Process and Reality*, cf. pp. 54, 72, 165, 366, 373, 423, 524.
[5] *Ibid.*, p. 29.

conforms in any particular instance, has its reason *either* in the character of some actual entity in the actual world of that concrescence, *or* in the character of the subject which is in process of concrescence. This category of explanation is termed the 'ontological principle.' It could also be termed the 'principle of efficient and final causation.' This ontological principle means that actual entities are the only *reasons;* so that to search for a *reason* is to search for one or more actual entities. It follows that any condition to be satisfied by one actual entity in its process expresses a fact either about the 'real internal constitutions' of some other actual entities, or about the 'subjective aim' conditioning that process."[6]

or again:

"According to the ontological principle there is nothing which floats into the world from nowhere. Everything in the actual world is referable to some actual entity. It is either transmitted from an actual entity in the past, or belongs to the subjective aim of the actual entity to whose concrescence it belongs . . ."[7]

This 'ontological principle' is found again and again in Whitehead's philosophy. It amounts to this, since everything, from God to the smallest item in the universe, is an actual entity, the ultimate explanation, the sufficient reason of all, is to be found in the actual entity.

The Principle of Relativity may be thus formulated: 'Although every entity is in potency to become all things, it is actually one specific thing.' As Whitehead words it:

"That the potentiality for being an element in a real concrescence of many entities into one actuality, is the one general metaphysical character attaching to all entities, actual and non-actual; and that every item in its universe is involved in each concrescence. In other words, it belongs to the nature of a 'being' that it is a potential for every 'becoming.' This is the 'principle of relativity'."[8]

This has its intrinsic relation with 'eternal objects,' which are pure potentialities, forms which guide the process of actual entities. 'Eternal objects' also have a relation with the Principle of Process, which principle expresses the definiteness of specific actual entities.

---

[6] *Process and Reality*, p. 36. The italics in this and subsequent citations are Whitehead's, unless otherwise noted.
[7] *Ibid.*, p. 373.
[8] *Ibid.*, p. 33.

The Principle of Process. This may be formulated as: 'The mode of becoming of any entity is the determining factor as to the mode of its existence.' In Whitehead's own words:

> "That *how* an actual entity *becomes* constitutes *what* that actual entity *is;* so that the two descriptions of an actual entity are not independent. Its 'being' is constituted by its 'becoming.' This is the 'principle of process.'"⁹

We shall meet this principle again when we consider the ingression of 'eternal objects' into actual entities.

Of these four principles, the most important is the Ontological Principle, for it is Whitehead's principle of sufficient reason. Since it is such, and since Whitehead has said that there is no going beyond the actual entity for the reasons of things, we shall center this investigation into Whitehead's theory of being and becoming about the actual entity. In the actual entity and in 'creativity' (which Whitehead calls the Category of the Ultimate) we find Whitehead's proposed explanation of the One and the Many. We find him explaining, through these two postulates, how reality is one and yet how reality is many. It is not so strange that a dynamic monism would advance an explanation of the One and Many, for any philosophy must try explain the plurality in reality. Whitehead does so, and we must remember that it is his professed intention to found a philosophy that transcends the specialized sciences.

The final realities out of which the world is made, the final units of reality, are actual entities. The world is an harmonious interplay of actual entities. Everything that exists is an actual entity, even God. What, then, are actual entities? Whitehead has defined them as follows:

> "An occasion (i.e., an actual entity) is a concretion—that is, a growing together—of diverse elements; that is why each occasion is an organism."¹⁰

This definition is enlarged by the following description:

> "(Actual entities) . . . are the final real things of which the world is made up. There is no going behind actual entities to find anything more real. They differ among themselves; God is an actual entity, and so is

---
⁹ *Ibid.*, p. 34.
¹⁰ *Ibid.*, p. 340; the parenthetical insertion is mine.

the most trivial puff of existence in far-off empty space. But though there are gradations of importance, and diversities of function, yet in the principles which actuality exemplifies all are on the same level. The final facts are, all alike, actual entities; and these actual entities are drops of experience, complete and interdependent."[11]

There is no going behind the actual occasion, as said above, for:

"The actual world is a process, and that the process is a becoming of actual entities. Thus actual entities are creatures; they are also termed 'actual occasions.'"[12]

If, then, the world, reality, is a process and the process is the becoming of actual entities, what is the actual entity in its analysis? We know that it is the basic and ultimate existent reality. It is the individual thing, and every individual thing, from God to the most remote and slight entity that exists, is an actual entity. In its essence, the actual entity is a 'concrescence,' a growing together. In asking the obvious question, "What grows together?" we can keep the same formal notion of the essence of the actual occasion; keep the same point of view, of concrescence, and consider the nature and mode of this growing together.

In analyzing the actual entity we find:

"That the first analysis of an actual entity, into its most concrete elements, discloses it to be a concrescence of prehensions, which have originated in its process of becoming. All further analysis is an analysis of prehensions."[13]

Prehensions are the equivalent of our 'natural appetites,' or natural tendencies. Hence an actual entity is a growing together of natural appetites or tendencies. We can begin to notice the element of formality with the postulation of natural tendencies. We can begin to see principles of process ('how an actual entity becomes constitutes what an actual entity is') and relativity (that an entity is in potency to prehend any and every other entity but actually prehends only those to which it has an affinity). Each prehension (which, we must remember, is an active process) consists of three factors:

". . . (a) the 'subject' which is prehending, namely, the

---
[11] *Ibid.*, p. 28.
[12] *Ibid.*, p. 33.
[13] *Ibid.*, p. 35.

actual entity in which that prehension is a concrete element; (b) the 'datum' which is prehended; (c) the 'subjective form' which is *how* that subject prehends that datum."[14]

Prehensions themselves are twofold:

"... (a) 'positive prehensions' which are termed 'feelings,' and (b) 'negative prehensions' which are said to eliminate from feeling."[15]

That is to say, these natural tendencies are either those of mutual attraction or of mutual repulsion. Furthermore, these prehensions are physical if they are among physical entities and 'conceptual' if they are between an actual entity and an 'eternal object,' that is, when an actual entity takes on a new form, or more properly, when a new form (an eternal object) enters the actual event by 'ingression.'

The relations between entities, whereby they exist in union with the rest of the universe, is termed a 'nexus'[16] and the uniting of these entities into a 'nexus' is a 'proposition.' It is also termed an 'objectification.'[17] It is thus termed because both or all entities make themselves objects of their mutual feelings.

Now, let us simplify all of the above, by way of a brief review. The entire world is a process. All of reality is a process, which process is the becoming of actual events, the ultimate units of reality. These units are constantly forming themselves into relations with other entities and with the entire universe. They do so according to their essence, which essences are individual units of growing together. This growing together, and this forming of relations with other entities, operates according to natural attractions ('positive prehensions' or 'feelings') and natural repulsions ('negative prehensions'). These attractions and repulsions are governed by the subjective form, which is the 'howness' of the entities.

We may illustrate the above with an example. A subject (let us call it Occasion A) is in potency to unite with every other entity in the world. It is continuously offering natural tendencies and natural repulsions. The tendencies are attractions towards any receptive entity, while the repulsions fend off any unattractive

---

[14] *Ibid.*, p. 35.
[15] *Ibid.*, p. 35.
[16] *Ibid.*, p. 32.
[17] *Ibid.*, p. 35.

entity. It encounters an attractive entity (Occasion B). It accepts the tendencies of the latter, while the latter accepts the tendencies of Occasion A. The repulsions of both ward off any interference with the process in order to guarantee its completion.

From what has been said above, it is obvious that Whitehead holds that the essence of each actual entity, and hence, the essence of all reality, composed as it is of actual essences, is activity. He claims the philosophical authority of Plato for this. In a passage in the *Sophist* Plato has said, in arguing against the static monism of Parmenides, "I hold that the definition of being is simply power."[18] Whitehead, commenting upon this, says:

> "Plato says that it is the *definition* of being that it exert power and be subject to the exertion of power. This means that the essence of being is to be implicated in causal action on other beings. It is the doctrine of Law as immanent. Furthermore a few sentences later he proceeds: '... being, as being known, is acted on by knowledge, and is therefore in motion, for that which is in a state of rest cannot be acted upon as we affirm ... Can we imagine being to be devoid of life and mind, and to remain in awful unmeaningness an everlasting fixture?'
> "Notice that in this argument, that which is not acted upon is a fixture. Plato denies that being can be conceived 'in awful unmeaningness an everlasting fixture.' It is therefore acted upon. This agrees with his primary definition that 'being' is the agent in action, and the recipient of action."[19]

We might say, here and now, that is an extension of Plato's meaning. The rest of the dialogue the *Sophist* seems to maintain more that being must operate before it can be known. That is certainly true, for knowledge begins with awareness, and we become aware of things only through their operations and properties. Rather than saying that being *is* power, Plato would rather mean that being *has* power. After all, it was Plato who foreshadowed Aristotle's great contribution of potency and act. That shows that Plato had some notion of a distinction between action and a being which acts.

However, Whitehead does maintain that the essence of the actual event is activity. That is obvious from his definition of it

---

[18] Plato, *The Sophist*, p. 247 (Jowett translation).
[19] Whitehead, *Adventures of Ideas*, pp. 153, 154.

as a 'concrescence,' or a growing together. As we shall see in the next chapter on Whitehead's philosophy of causality, this concrescence takes on the note of self-causation, self-creation.

What we have seen so far is only one side of the scheme, the world of activity composed of actual events. There is the other side, the world of 'eternal objects.' These too are entities, but of a different sort. These 'eternal objects' are defined as:

"Pure Potentials for the Specific Determination of Fact, or Forms of Definiteness."[20]

The purpose of 'eternal objects' is to give formal unity and identity to actual entities, which would otherwise tend to be chaotic. Thus they are forms of definiteness, themselves conceptual, awaiting ingression into the ever-progressive process that is the world. There are lesser forms in the actual entity, such as emotions, valuations, purposes, adversions, consciousness,[21] but these are what we would term accidental forms, forms of properties and operations, not forms of essence. The forms of essence are the eternal objects. Actual entities and eternal objects are the two basic realities out of which the world is a cosmos and not a chaos. As Whitehead says:

"That the fundamental types of entities are actual entities and eternal objects; and that the other types of entities only express how all entities of the two fundamental types are in community with each other, in the actual world."[22]

Whitehead claims to be a Platonist. He said that the history of philosophy is a series of footnotes to Plato.[23] Whitehead is greatly enamored of Plato's world of ideals, and this is his modern version of it, a substitution of eternal objects for Platonic forms.

"Accordingly, by way of employing a term devoid of misleading suggestions, I use the phrase 'eternal objects' for what in the preceding paragraph of this section I have termed a 'Platonic form' "[24]

Where do these eternal objects subsist? In the mind of God, in what we shall later see is termed the 'primordial nature' of God.

---

[20] *Process and Reality*, p. 32.
[21] *Ibid.*, p. 33.
[22] *Ibid.*, p. 37.
[23] *Ibid.*, p. 63.
[24] *Ibid.*, p. 70.

It is this postulate of external forms residing in the mind of God that is the guarantee of the subsistence of ever-changing actual events.

> "The notion of 'subsistence' is merely the notion of how eternal objects can be components of the primordial nature of God. This is a question for subsequent discussion. But eternal objects, as in God's primordial nature, constitute the Platonic world of ideas."[25]

Whitehead, in his theodicy, is going to be consistent enough to follow his postulates as to the uniting of eternal objects with actual entities in the three following principles:

1. Actual entities and eternal objects actually unite in the primordial nature of God.
2. God thus undergoes process.
3. God is enriched with this process, gaining actuality whereas he was formerly merely conceptual.

So far, then, we have seen that reality consists of the world of actual entities crossing the world of ideals, of ideals entering into the actual entities for the formation of new entities. At this union of the two, the new actual entity gains its 'initial phase,' which is its direction towards its end, and undergoes a process of self growing together, self-creation, self-causation, by means of its positive and negative prehensions. This process goes on in God, in whom the eternal objects reside. It is the crossing of two worlds, the world of activity, pure becoming, and the world of eternal objects, which reside in God. Thus, it is God entering into the world, God enriching the world, God being enriched by the world. We may note the resemblance to Hegel's philosophy as found in the philosophy of Whitehead.

Whitehead had said that the ultimate explanation, the sufficient reason of all reality, is to be found in the actual entity. He also said that the actual entity is a growing together. Now, what is the principle explanatory of this growing together? Whitehead calls it the Category of the Ultimate, and terms it 'creativity.' He defines it and describes it in the following words:

> " 'Creativity' is the universal of universals characterizing ultimate matter of fact. It is that ultimate principle by which the many which are the universe disjunctively become the one actual occasion, which is the universe

---
[25] *Ibid.*, p. 73.

conjunctively. It lies in the nature of things that the many enter into complex unity. . . .

". . . . The ultimate metaphysical principle is the advance from disjunction to conjunction, creating a novel entity other than the entities given in disjunction. . . . The many become one and are increased by one. In their natures, entities are disjunctively 'many' in process of passage into conjunctive unity. This Category of the Ultimate replaces Aristotle's category of 'primary substance.'"[26]

This is Whitehead's explanation of the problem of the One and the Many. The actual entities are the Many. The principle whereby the Many become One is creativity, and creativity is the ultimate principle uniting the Many into the One. For the sake of clarity, we might say that this is the opposite view of Aristotelianism and Thomism (and, we might say, the opposite of Plato's *Timaeus*). Aristotle and St. Thomas would view the problem of the One and the Many as one of the differentiation of being. Whitehead considers it the unification of becoming.

This is also a clear indication of the dynamic monism in his philosophy. His ultimate principle, his substitute for substance, is a form of becoming, creativity. It even takes precedence over God. As he says at the beginning of *Process and Reality:*

"In the philosophy of organism, this ultimate is termed 'creativity'; and God is its primordial, non-temporal accident."[27]

Even God is subject to creativity. Through creativity, God is united to the world and the world is conjoined to him. The following diagram may perhaps clarify this process where, through the joining of eternal objects to actual entities in the primordial nature of God, creativity unites what is disjoined; where God enters the world, guides the processes of the world, and is enriched by the world while the world is enriched in him.

What is the final outcome of all reality, of all this conjunction? It is the 'satisfaction' of each entity (God included) in the complete acquisition of each actual entity (again, God included) of thorough union with all of reality. To quote Whitehead:

"The actual entity terminates its becoming in one complex feeling involving a completely determinate bond

---
[26] *Process and Reality*, pp. 31, 32.
[27] *Ibid.*, p. 10.

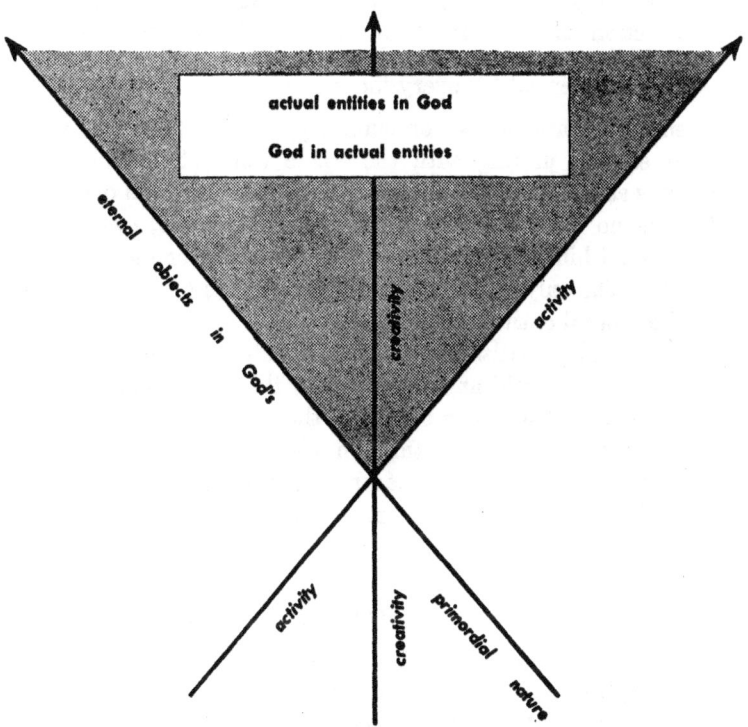

with every item in the universe, the bond being either a positive or a negative prehension. This termination is the 'satisfaction' of the actual entity."[28]

But when this state arrives, does the actual entity become a being? Does it arrive at a state of rest? Does the universe come to a full stop? No, for two reasons:

1. In the course of time, actual entities arrive at the state of satisfaction at different times. They do not arrive at satisfaction simultaneously.

2. When the actual entity arrives at satisfaction, it becomes a potential for every becoming.

"This is the doctrine of the emergent unity of the superject. An actual entity is to be conceived both as a subject presiding over its own immediacy of becoming,

---
[28] *Process and Reality*, p. 71.

and a superject which is the atomic creature exercising its function of objective immortality. It has become a 'being'; and it belongs to the nature of every 'being' that it is a potential for every 'becoming.'"[29]

Hence, the process goes on endlessly, and the process is that of actual entities uniting with the whole world, becoming beings, and thus as potentials, entering in the process over and over again. There is no stop, no rest. Every eternal object, every actual entity, God himself, all are components of the one great reality, process. The only difference is that God is non-temporal, whereas all other actual entities are temporal.

The arrival at satisfaction, the complete union of each entity with the entire world and with God in the world is its 'objective immortality.' It is not immortal in the sense that it lives *as such* forever, but that it passes through a series of transmigrations in its absorption in God. We may note the dynamic counterpart to Spinoza's static immortality, immersion and absorption into God. We may also note the Platonic poetic vision in that things change but remain forever.

SUMMARY

1. The actual world, all reality, is a process. Process ('creativity') is the ultimate principle.
2. This process is (i) the uniting of the components of the actual entity; (ii) the uniting of eternal object to actual entity; (iii) the uniting of actual entity to actual entity.
3. This is accomplished, under the principle of creativity, in the crossing of the two worlds, the world of activity and the world of eternal objects.
4. Since the eternal objects subsist in the primordial nature of God, the process takes place in the primordial nature of God.
5. Thus, the world is united to God by God's entering into the world.
6. When each entity attains its satisfaction, it is a potential for every other becoming. Thus, in its renascence, it attains its objective immortality.
7. Since every temporal actual entity reaches its satisfaction, and since no actual entities reach satisfaction simultaneously, the process goes on forever.

---

[29] *Ibid.*, p. 71. Note the return to the Principle of Relativity.

CHAPTER IV

WHITEHEAD'S EXPLANATION OF CAUSALITY

The purpose of this chapter is not so much to prove that Professor Whitehead believes in causality as to investigate his notion and explanation of causality. Whitehead speaks almost constantly of causality, and makes much use of the term 'efficient causation' and 'final causation.' Explicit in his doctrine is a notion of formal causality, consequent to his doctrine on eternal objects.

Whitehead explicitly states his belief in causality in the following words:

> "In the first place, there can be no living science unless there is a widespread instinctive conviction of the existence of an *Order of Things*, and, in particular, of an *Order of Nature*. I have used the word *instinctive* advisedly. It does not matter what men say in words, so long as their activities are controlled by settled instincts. . . . This remark is important in respect to the history of scientific thought. For we shall find that since the time of Hume, the fashionable scientific philosophy has been such as to deny the rationality of science. . . . If the cause in itself discloses no information as to the effect, so that the first invention of it must be *entirely* arbitrary, it follows at once that science is impossible, except in the sense of establishing *entirely arbitrary* connections which are not warranted by anything intrinsic to the natures either of causes or effects."[1]

In that citation, we note the following points: (i) the necessary connection between order, the order of nature, and causality; (ii) the instinctive recognition of causality; (iii) the necessary connection between cause and effect; (iv) the necessary connection between knowledge (science) and causality. If there is no causality, then science becomes an entirely arbitrary system of hypotheses.

Hence Whitehead holds that causality is an objective something taken as a matter of fact. And in differing with Hume, as he here does, we would suppose that he would uphold the validity of objective causality. However, in his writings, we meet a difficulty. It seems to be only an apparent difficulty due to the nature of

---

[1] *Science and the Modern World*, p. 5.

organic philosophy and Whitehead's peculiar use of terms. However, it calls for investigation.

In *Adventures of Ideas,* Whitehead spends a chapter arguing that cause is recognized instinctively, through association of memories and past experience, rather than recognized in objective events. Here he bases himself largely upon Hume, and remarks:

> "... The conclusion follows that there is an observed relation of causation between such occasions. The general character of this observed relation explains at once memory and personal identity. They are all different aspects of the doctrine of immanence of occasions of experience. The additional conclusion can also be derived, that insofar as we apply notions of causation to the understanding of events of nature, we must conceive these events under the general notions which apply to occasions of experience. For we can only understand causation in terms of our observations of these occasions. This appeal to Hume has the sole purpose of illustrating the common-sense obviousness of the present thesis."[2]

Furthermore, Whitehead seems to be quite subjective, as was Hume, in other matters. For example, he remarks,

> "In other words, the order of nature cannot be justified by the mere observation of nature. For there is nothing in the present fact which inherently refers either to the past or the future. It looks, therefore, as though memory, as well as induction, would fail to find any justification within nature itself. ... The only wonder is that the world did in fact wait for Hume before noting the difficulty."[3]

Much on the same subject, he adds, "Thus the bodies are perceived as with qualities which in fact are purely the offspring of the mind. Thus, nature gets credit which should in truth be reserved for ourselves: the rose for its scent; the nightingale for his song, and the sun for his radiance."[4]

Whitehead's conclusion to all this would seem to be that although there is causality, we cannot recognize it. We have to take it instinctively. Yet without causality, science is purely arbitrary. We cannot even observe the order of nature through simple observation. Hence, the instinctiveness of causality apparently

---
[2] *Adventures of Ideas,* p. 237.
[3] *Science and the Modern World,* p. 73.
[4] *Ibid.,* p. 77.

does not mean observation of a self evident fact. Instead, it seems to be the force of memory of past experiences applied to concrete reality. In other words, it seems as though we cannot know causality, but we must act upon it, for any kind of order.

However, as remarked before, this objection seems only apparent, for Whitehead has, as we have seen, a doctrine on 'Symbolic Reference' which postulates objective causality of our knowledge.

Whitehead bases himself upon experience for the fact of causality. In keeping with his philosophy of organism, he maintains that even though we do project our notion of causality from our ideas, that does not mean that our ideas cause objective causality. Instead, our idea of causality is the effect of objective causality. In fact, he even dislikes the term 'project' since that would give the impression that we apply our a priori idea of causality to succession. In this he is flatly and expressly against Hume and Kant, who both agree on causality. He maintains that our mind clarifies objective causality, but presupposes it. That is the whole point to his doctrine on 'Symbolic Reference,' which is as close as he comes to an ex professo treatise on epistemology. The very fact that he rejects subjective epistemology as we understand it, is on the grounds that in the philosophy of organism there is only one substance, and not a world of things divorced from a world of ideals. In this he is not only reflecting the monadology of Leibniz, but he is also adapting the atomism of the ancient Greeks.

He starts out by considering our idea as the 'supplemental phase' of perception, and says:

> "The supplemental phase lifts the presented duration into vivid distinctness, so that the vague efficacity of the indistinct external world in the immediate past is precipitated upon the representative regions in the contemporary present. In the usual language, the sensations are projected. This phraseology is unfortunate; for there never were sensations apart from these geometrical relations."[5]

With that background, Whitehead stoutly maintains that Kant and Hume have the order of things reversed in the perception of causation.

> "The discussion of the problem, constituted by the connection between causation and perception, has been

---

[5] *Process and Reality*, p. 262.

conducted by the various schools of thought derived from Hume and Kant under the misapprehension generated by an inversion of the true constitution of experience. The inversion was explicit in the writings of Hume and Kant: for both of them, presentational immediacy was the primary fact of perception, and any apprehension of causation was, somehow or other, to be elicited from this primary fact. . . . The Philosophy of Organism does not admit its truth, and thus rejects the touchstone which is the neolithic weapon of 'critical' philosophy. It must be remembered that clearness in consciousness is no evidence for primitiveness in the genetic process: the opposite doctrine is more nearly true."[6]

Then, in an appeal to experience, whereupon he takes the empiricists on their own ground (". . . but, after all, it is the empiricists who began this appeal to Caesar . . .")[7] Whitehead considers the ordinary phenomenon of the sudden turning on of an electric light in a dark room causing a man's eyes to blink. According to Hume, the response to such a stimulus would be nothing other than the "response to presentational immediacy,"[8] that is, to an a priori habit. Whitehead turns to the physiology involved, and shows that, biologically, the blinking is nothing other than the effect caused by the action of the light upon the nerves of the eye. It is fundamentally causality, for "this physiological explanation is couched wholly in terms of causal efficacy."[9] Then he goes on to consider it from the man's point of view. The man will recognize the causality involved, namely, the light as the cause, and the blinking of the eyes as the effect. When asked about it, "the man will explain his experience by saying, 'The flash made me blink;' and if his statement be doubted, he will reply: 'I know it, because I felt it.'"[10]

Although the philosophy of organism will accept the man's statement, Hume would try to explain that what the man felt was a habit of blinking after flashes. Whereupon, Whitehead counters, "But how can a 'habit' be felt, when a 'cause' cannot be felt? Is there any presentational immediacy in the feeling of a 'habit'?

---

[6] *Process and Reality*, p. 263.
[7] *Ibid.*, p. 263.
[8] *Ibid.*, p. 264.
[9] *Ibid.*, p. 265.
[10] *Ibid.*, p. 266.

Hume by a sleight of hand confuses a 'habit of feeling blinks after flashes' with a *'feeling of the habit* of feeling blinks after flashes.' . . . The notion of causation arose because mankind lives amid experiences in the mode of causal efficacity."[11]

Whitehead goes on to show that even where there is no case of conscious recognition, there is still causation, response to stimuli, etc. His basis for that in his own philosophy is that feeling is everywhere, in everything, and, as we shall see, feeling is causation. Hence, there is causation everywhere and in everything.[12]

Whitehead's basing causality upon experience is well summarized in the following words:

> "Hume's doctrine inverts this relationship by making causal efficacy, as an experience, dependent upon presentational immediacy. This doctrine, whatever be its merits, is not based upon any appeal to experience."[13]

The above is taken from Whitehead's theory of knowledge, wherein he postulates that our knowledge is *truly caused* by external things operating on the sense organs. It is the basis of his recognition of causality among extra-mental entities. Whitehead maintains that we directly perceive the external world, and in it, causality. We clarify our notions of what we experience through the memory of past experience. We here and now perceive causality as a phenomenon, through the senses. We clarify it and understand it through the mind. We do *not* project the notion of causality into sequence, as do Kant and Hume. We recognize it.

Hence, when Whitehead would congratulate man for his perception of the sweetness of the rose, he is not congratulating man for being the cause of that sweetness, as though it were a creation of the mind, as Hume and Kant would say. He is congratulating man for having and using mental equipment to clarify the effect of recognizing what is in the objective datum. That is far closer to Scholasticism than to Kantianism.

In the same way, I think we should interpret Whitehead's use of the term, 'intuitiveness' in causality. As we have seen, Whitehead holds causality to be intuitive. What I think he means is that it is self evident from experience. We hold that causality

---

[11] *Ibid.*, p. 266.
[12] *Ibid.*, p. 268.
[13] *Ibid.*, p. 267.

is intuitive in that way. It is something we cannot help but recognize, since all experience is based upon it. Whitehead has the same view of experience, and I would be inclined to think that his notion of intuitive causality is close to ours.

However, even though in his treatment of causality Whitehead uses many terms and many ideas which strike us as being very close to Thomism, we must remember that Whitehead's point of view is always that of a constant flux, and any of his theories are always in terms of 'actual occasions,' 'prehensions,' 'concrescences,' etc. In other words, causality for Whitehead seems to be postulated as another manifestation of the great and somewhat orderly change necessitated by the philosophy of organism.

I. *The Fact of Causality*

The gradation of beings in Whitehead's philosophy is according to high-grade and low-grade actual entities in societies. According to Whitehead these societies must have a reason for their existence as such, for:

> "That each entity in the universe of a given concrescence *can*, as far as its own nature is concerned, be implicated in that concrescence in one or other of many bodies; but *in fact* it is implicated only in *one* mode:..."[14]

In other words, there is a distinction between the actual entity as potential, or possible, and the actual entity as actual. "This indetermination, rendered determinate in the real concrescence, is the meaning of 'Potentiality'. It is a *conditioned* indetermination, and is therefore called a *real* potentiality."[15]

A more explicit statement of the fact of the reason of societies is as follows: "The point of a 'society' as the term is here used, is that it is self-sustaining; in other words, that it is its own reason."[16] Or again, "A society has an essential character, whereby it is the society that it is . . ."[17]

Those statements, involving as they do, the potential and actual, are his restatement of the actual entity as the principle of sufficient reason, again the Ontological Principle. They state in so many words that every society or actual entity can, potentially, have been composed of any actual occasions but that de facto, they

---

[14] *Process and Reality*, p. 34.
[15] *Ibid*, p. 34.
[16] *Ibid*., p. 261.
[17] *Ibid*., p. 262.

are not. They have an 'essential character' preventing that. They are their own reasons, and that flows from their nature as concretions, for the indeterminate is made determinate in the concrescence. This involves all that has been said in the chapter on Being and Becoming about 'prehensions', 'data,' 'feelings', etc., and hinges around the fact, as also mentioned before, that how an actual entity becomes constitutes what that actual entity is.

However, there is more to it than that. The very notion of society being what it is involved another idea, that of 'immanence.' "The self-identity of a society is founded upon the self-identity of its defining characteristic, and upon the mutual immanence of its occasions."[18] 'Defining characteristic' immediately suggests formality, about which we shall see later. Now we shall consider 'immanence,' in which, I think, we find the key to efficiency and finality.

In discussing immanence, we must regret, in this instance, the lack of definition in Whitehead's works. He describes immanence, explains its function to a certain extent, but scarcely defines. However, after reading Chapter VIII (*Cosmology*), XI (*Objects and Subjects*), and XII (*Past, Present, and Future*) of *Adventures of Ideas*,[19] and in the light of the following citations, we come to the conclusion that immanence is the action of the past on the present. The first lines of Chapter XII are:

> "The doctrine of immanence of past occasions in the occasions which are future, relatively to them, has been sufficiently discussed in the last chapter."[20]

The previous chapter had dealt with *Objects and Subjects*, and presupposed Chapter VII, on *Cosmology*, wherein Whitehead had shown the part of the atomism of Lucretius and Democritus, of certain sections of Plato's dialogues, and of the monadology of Leibniz, in the philosophy of organism. Continuing the quotation he says:

> "The past has an objective existence in the present which lies in the future beyond itself."[21]

Then he goes on to show that just as the past exercises in the present, so does the present exercise in the future. Once again, it

---

[18] *Adventures of Ideas*, p. 262 ff.
[19] *Ibid.*, pp. 152–178; 225–257.
[20] *Ibid.*, p. 246.
[21] *Ibid.*, p. 259.

is the doctrine of constant flux in organism, but causality has reference from past to present to future and not among contemporaries. He hints at that when he says, "The idea of temporal transition can never be wholly disengaged from that of 'causation.' This latter notion is merely a special way of considering direct immanence of the past its future."²² He says it more explicitly in the following quotation:

> "For apart from contemporaries, one occasion will be in the future of the other. Thus the earlier will be immanent in the later according to the mode of efficient causality, and the later in the earlier according to the mode of anticipation . . ."²³

With relation to finality in immanence, he says:

> "Whether the ideas thus introduced by the novel conceptual prehension be old or new, they have this decisive result, that the occasion arises as an effect facing its past and ends as a cause facing its future. In between there lies the teleology of the universe."²⁴

Concerning contemporary events, he writes: "It is the definition of contemporary events that they happen in causal independence of each other."²⁵ Why? Because:

> "Thus two contemporary occasions are such that neither belongs to the past of the other. The two occasions are not in any direct relation of efficient causation."²⁶

The result is that the "Vast causal independence of contemporary occasions is the preservative of the elbow-room of the Universe. It provides each actuality with a welcome environment for irresponsibility. . . . Our claim for freedom is rooted in our relationship to our contemporary environment. Nature does provide a field for independent activities. The understanding of the Universe requires that we conceive in their proper relations to each other the various roles, of efficient causation, of teleological self-creation, and of contemporary independence."²⁷

Specifically, then, the fact of causality is to be found in the immanence of the past in the present, in the concrescences of

---

²² *Adventures of Ideas*, p. 259.
²³ *Ibid.*, p. 259.
²⁴ *Ibid.*, p. 254.
²⁵ *Ibid.*, p. 251.
²⁶ *Ibid.*, p. 251.
²⁷ *Ibid.*, p. 251.

things, which are temporal. It is, in fact, process, the becoming of new entities. The very becoming of them is causation, and specifically, efficient and final causation. Formal causation seems to be necessary in process, since, as we have seen before, there are definite modes of process consequent to the impression of eternal objects into actual entities and as a matter of fact, every actual entity does not combine with any or every other actual occasion because of those definite modes of process. That formal aspect seems to be the 'defining characteristic' of immanence.[28] Causality is temporal, from past to present to future. Contemporaneousness is free, for contemporaries are not causes of one another, but causes of future entities.

Before passing on from the fact of causality to the nature of causality, we can summarize the fact of causality in the following quotation:

> "That every condition to which the process of becoming conforms in any particular instance, has its reason *either* in the character of some actual entity in the actual world of that concrescence, *or* in the character of the subject which is in process of concrescence. This category of explanation is termed the 'ontological principle.' It could also be termed the 'principle of efficient and final causation.' This ontological principle means that the actual entities are the only *reasons* so that to search for a *reason* is to search for one or more actual entities. It follows that any condition to be satisfied by one actual entity in its process expresses a fact either about the 'real internal constitutions' of some other actual entities, or about the 'subjective aim' conditioning that process."[29]

II. *The Nature of Causality*

The above quotation serves as an excellent transition from the fact of causality to the nature of causality, since it contains self-causation, which as we shall see is final cause, and other-causation, which as we shall also see is efficient cause.

The first thing to note, now, from the above quotation and from the fact that the philosophy of organism is a philosophy of change, is the fact that causality, in any of its aspects, is simply a specific application of the general tenets of organism (at least in theory) to the becoming of occasions.

---

[28] *Ibid.*, p. 262.
[29] *Ibid.*, p. 262.

Change and causality are being. As we have seen, Whitehead claims to base himself on Plato for this. Plato had said, "... I hold that the definition of being is simply power."[30] To which Whitehead adds:

"... Plato says that it is the *definition* of being that it exert power and be subject to the exertion of power. This means that the essence of being is to be implicated in causal action or other beings. It is the doctrine of Law as immanent. Further, a few sentences later he proceeds: '... being, as being known, is acted on by knowledge, and is therefore in motion, for that which is in a state of rest cannot be acted upon as we affirm.... Can we imagine being to be devoid of life and mind, and to remain in awful unmeaningness an everlasting fixture.'

"Notice that in this argument, that which is not acted upon is a fixture. Plato denies that being can be conceived 'in awful unmeaningness an everlasting fixture.' It is therefore acted upon. This agrees with his primary definition that 'being' is the agent in action, and the recipient of action."[31]

Now since action and reaction are the essence of being, it follows that concrescence and prehension are the essence of being. But prehension immediately suggests causality, and in fact, positive prehensions, or feelings are causes, for "A simple physical feeling is an act of causation."[32] Hence, in a certain sense, being is causality. What kind of causality? We may consider the following quotations to decide that:

"In the philosophy of organism it is not 'substance' which is permanent, but 'form'. Forms suffer changing relations; actual entities 'perpetually perish' subjectively, but are immortal objectively. Actuality in perishing acquires objectivity, while it loses subjective immediacy. It loses the final causation which is its internal principle of unrest, and it acquires efficient causation whereby it is a ground of obligation characterizing the creativity."[33]

Again, and a bit more concisely:

"It belongs to the essence of this subject that it pass into objective immortality. Thus its own constitution

---

[30] Plato, *The Sophist*, p. 247 (Jowett's translation).
[31] *Adventures of Ideas*, pp. 153, 154.
[32] *Process and Reality*, p. 44.
[33] *Ibid.*, p. 361.

involves that its own activity in *self*-formation passes into its activity of *other*-formation."[34]

Causality, then, is a twofold process of self-formation and otherformation. In all of this, final causality is the principle of unrest, the seeking of stability, and hence, finality has an intransic part in all of process.

Now a fundamental postulate in all of process, and which plays an intimate role in finality, is the 'subjective aim' resulting from the impression of eternal objects into actual entities "which controls the becoming of a subject, is that subject feeling a proposition with the subjective form of purpose to realize it in that process of self-creation."[35] The subjective aim has the following role of finality:

"The subjective aim is this subject itself determining its own self-creation as one creature."[36]

Furthermore, "The 'subjective aim' at 'satisfaction' constitutes the final cause, or lure, whereby there is determinate concrescence; and that attained 'satisfaction' remains as an element in the content of creative purpose."[37] In fact, Whitehead says in so many words that:

"Concrescence moves towards its final cause, which is its subjective aim;..."[38]

Now, since process is reality, and since concrescences are actual entities as well as the production of actual entities,[39] we reach the conclusion that finality, according or Whitehead, is determinate self-creation, self-perfection. It is the principle of unrest, the process of self-creation, the striving for self-perfection, or satisfaction. When this satisfaction is reached, final causation is lost, for the end is reached, and the actual entity gains efficient causality.

We must note that the efficient causality thus attained does not fill the role of educing form from matter. After all, forms are extrinsic, and a dynamic philosophy allows for no matter.

---

[34] *Adventures of Ideas*, p. 248.
[35] *Process and Reality*, p. 37.
[36] *Ibid.*, p. 108.
[37] *Ibid.*, p. 137.
[38] *Ibid.*, p. 320.
[39] *Ibid.*, p. 44.

> "If the subject-predicate form of statement be taken to be metaphysically ultimate, it is then impossible to express this doctrine of feelings and their superject. It is better to say that they *are aimed at* their subject. For the latter mode of expression removes the subject from the scope of the feelings and assigns it to an external agency. Thus the feeling would be wrongly abstracted from its own final cause. This final cause is an inherent element in the feeling, constituting the unity of that feeling. An actual entity feels as it does feel in order to be the actual entity which it is. In this way an actual entity satisfies Spinoza's notion of substance: it is *causa sui*. The creativity is not an external agency with its own ulterior purposes. All actual entities share with God the characteristic of transcending all other actual entities, including God. The universe is thus a creative advance into novelty. The alternative to this doctrine is a static morphological universe."[40]

Thus we can say that for Whitehead, causality par excellence is final causality, since self-causation is a fundamental tenet in his philosophy of organism, and self-causation depends upon finality.

Self-causation does not mean that the entity reaches its end by itself. That would be against the very nature of organic philosophy, which presupposes a constant flux of interaction of those things which have the same past, or which influence each other. The actual entity receives help in attaining its end, and that help is the whole world.

> "The deterministic efficient causation is the inflow of the actual world in its own proper character of its own feelings, with their own intensive strength, felt and re-enacted by the novel concrescent subject."[41]

Hence, efficient causality is the help given by the other actual entities in any actual occasion's attaining of its end. It is the contribution that is given to an actual entity in attaining satisfaction. It is 'other formation,' and it is the completion of self-perfection.

> "Thus its own constitution involves that its own activity in *self*-formation passes into its activity of other-formation."[42]

---

[40] *Process and Reality*, p. 339.
[41] *Ibid.*, p. 374.
[42] *Adventures of Ideas*, p. 248.

We must note here, though, that an entity must be completely self caused; it must have attained its final end before it becomes an efficient cause. That means that in the past it must have passed into satisfaction. Now, in the present, it exercises efficiency, and that, apparently, is what Whitehead means when he says that efficiency is the past operating on the present, or the present operating on the future.

To make more clear what Whitehead postulates as regards the interaction of efficiency and finality, we must look somewhat into the process of causality.

Causality, as mentioned before, has to do with feelings. Feelings are described as follows:

> "A feeling—i.e., a positive prehension—is essentially a transition effecting a concrescence...."[43]

that is, a transition effecting or causing an actual occasion.

> "... Its complex constitution is analysable into five factors which express what that transition consists of and effects. The factors are: (i) the 'subject' which feels, (ii) the 'initial data' which are to be felt, (iii) the 'elimination' in virtue of negative prehensions, (iv) the 'objective datum' which is felt, (v) the 'subjective form' which is *how* that subject feels that objective datum."[44]

The 'subject,' we must remember, is that which is to cause itself, hence it is that which is seeking finality, which is in a state of unrest.

The subject, in seeking its finality, following its subjective aim, feels the initial data, for self creation. We might also say, that the data feel the subject for efficient creation. The feelings themselves "aim at the feeler, as their final cause. The feelings are what they are in order that their subject may be what it is."[45] The feelings aiming at the feeler, and being what they are in order that their subject may be what it is is according to the subjective aim, which, in the long run, constitutes what an actual entity will be. We again must remember that now an actual entity becomes determines what an actual entity will be. The 'howness' con-

---

[43] *Process and Reality*, p. 337.
[44] *Ibid.*, p. 337.
[45] *Ibid.*, p. 339.

stitutes the 'whatness.'[46] This determination by process is the result of subjective aim. Hence, before going into formality, we can see how Whitehead preserves the fact of experience that certain things act and are acted upon only by certain things. In self-creation, the becoming entity is so constituted that it will react, so to speak, or accept only certain data offered it in the manner of efficiency. It does that because of its subjective aim which works through the negative prehensions eliminating certain other data.

That leads to the question as to where the becoming entity gets its subjective aim, which is its principle of determination. It cannot come from nothing, so:

> "It derives from God its basic conceptual aim, relevant to its actual world, yet with indeterminations awaiting its own decisions. This subjective aim, in its successive modifications, remains the unifying factor governing the successive phases of interplay between physical and conceptual feelings."[47]

Thus, every actual entity derives from the eternal object in the primordial nature of God its basic conceptual aim. In striving to fulfill that aim, it is exercising final causality. In reaching that aim, it achieves satisfaction, and further perfects itself by becoming an efficient cause, helping other actual entities to achieve their satisfaction. The indeterminations that are with the basic subjective aim are left to be determined by its own decisions in Process.

Finality and formality are derived from eternal objects. Efficiency is the cooperation of the whole world, more specifically, adjacent actual entities, in the quest of finality, and satisfaction leads into efficient causality, whereby a thing, achieving objective immortality, exists for the cause of other beings. Now, since in objective immortality, an entity also remains a potential for what is analogous to its matter from the other entities that are objectively immortal, but derives its basic conceptual aim from God.

We can summarize up this section of efficiency and finality in the words of Whitehead, where he states the whole process:

> "If we prefer the phraseology, we can say that God and the actual world jointly constitute the character of the creativity for the initial phase of the novel concrescence.

---

[46] *Process and Reality*, p. 34.
[47] *Ibid.*, p. 343.

The subject thus constituted, is the autonomous master of its own subjective aim in the concrescence into superject with objective immortality. At any stage it is subject-superject. According to this explanation, self-determination is always imaginative in its origin. The deterministic efficient causation is the inflow of the actual world in its own proper character of its own feelings, with their own intensive strength, felt and re-enacted by the novel concrescent subject. But this re-enaction has a mere character of conformation to pattern. The subjective valuation is the work of novel conceptual feelings: and in proportion to its importance, acquired in complex processes of integration and reintegration, this autonomous conceptual element modifies the subjective forms throughout the whole range of feeling in that concrescence and thereby guides the integration."[48]

He expresses it more briefly in the following:

"According to this account, efficient causation expresses the transition from actual entity to actual entity; and final causation expresses the internal process whereby the actual entity becomes itself. . . . An actual entity is at once the product of the efficient past, and is, also, in Spinoza's phrase, *causa sui*."[49]

Hence, although efficient causation has some say in determination, it is auxiliary to the basic conceptual aim, which is final cause, and which has the primary say. Efficient cause, then, is external, while final causation is internal.

Form and formality are essential to the philosophy of organism. Off hand we can say that they have to be. In a constant flux characterized by constant change, there must be a principle of formality in all the entailing becoming to prevent chaos, and this principle is form. In fact, form is the one abiding reality in all this becoming. That is to be found in all of Whitehead's philosophy, and is presupposed throughout it.

"In the philosophy of organism, it is not 'substance' which is permanent, but 'form.'"[50]

In the light of that fundamental principle, we must interpret what Whitehead means when he says, speaking about 'feeling' in the process of concrescence or prehension:

---

[48] *Process and Reality*, p. 374.
[49] *Ibid.*, p. 228.
[50] *Ibid.*, p. 44.

> "Its complex constitution is analysable into . . . the 'subjective form' which is *how* that subject feels that objective datum."[51]
>
> "The subjective form receives its determination from the negative prehensions, the objective datum, and the conceptual origination of the subject. The negative prehensions are determined by the categorial conditions governing feelings, by the subjective form, and by the initial data. This mutual determination of the elements involved in a feeling is one expression of the truth that the subject of the feeling is a *causa sui*. . . . This mutual sensitivity of feelings in one subject, expresses the notion sensitivity of feelings in one subject, expresses the notion of final causation in the guise of pre-established harmony."[52]

Thus, all feeling and all transition, all determination in the final causation of an actual occasion, all interaction of efficiency and finality is according to a form, an external form, the eternal object. This causation according to form is formal causality in Whitehead's philosophy. And this, I think, is what we should understand when Whitehead says:

> ". . . and how an actual entity becomes constitutes what that actual entity is; so that the two descriptions of an actual entity are not independent. Its 'being' is constituted by its 'becoming.'"[53]

But here we must note that form is primarily an ingression into action. The basic conceptual aim, which, if anything, is the formal cause, is intrinsically connected with finality. Form, dealing as it does with process, seems to be a mode to prevent wrong concrescences and to guide correct ones. It is the guide for the correct resolution of the indetermination, that together with the basic conceptual aim, are present in the nascent entity in its initial phase.

Since Whitehead rejects substance, and therefore being, we could not very well expect him to hold to material cause. However, he does have something analogous to material cause, in the ground, or origin of the concrescent process.

> "The ground, or origin, of the concrescent process is

---

[51] *Process and Reality*, p. 338.
[52] *Ibid.*, p. 338.
[53] *Ibid.*, p. 34.

the multiplicity of data in the universe, actual entities and eternal objects and propositions and nexus."[54]

Out of these are made all things. These are the potentials out of which new entities become by the interplay of efficiency and finality according to forms, and that might very well be a summary of the philosophy of organism, namely, that out of the multiplicity of actual occasions,[55] unity might be achieved by the interplay of self-causation (finality) through other-causation (efficiency) according to forms.

SUMMARY

We can state, first of all, that Whitehead maintains causality. He maintains an intuitive recognition of objective causality, and is professedly opposed to Kant and Hume and their doctrines of a priori categories and habits applied to sequence or relation. His basis for this is experience, and he states that experience tells us that there is objective causality. Our notions of cause are the effects of objective causality working upon perception, or our 'presentational immediacy.' To state, as Hume does, that we perceive habits is to beg the question. If we can perceive habits, we can perceive causes, and to state that we perceive only habits does not answer the problem.

The only concession that he will grant the subjectivists is that the action of the mind is the action of clarifying an objective reality.

The process of causality is contained in his doctrine of concrescence, especially in feelings, which are causes. Causation is par excellence final causation for that is self-causation. A being receives its initial phase, which is its subjective aim, from eternal objects in the 'primordial nature' of God. The achievement of that subjective aim, or final causality, is through the feelings radiating from itself and felt from other actual entities. The help it receives from other entities is efficient causality, and external thing. Its intrinsic striving for that subjective aim—its principle of unrest—is its final cause. It achieves that end according to a set form, which is its formal cause. Its aim is derived from God. Its material being is derived from other actual entities which are what we would term its material cause.

---

[54] *Ibid.*, p. 343.
[55] *Ibid.*, p. 37.

The aim of final causality is self-causation and self-perfection. When that state is achieved, an entity loses its final causation, and becomes an efficient cause, helping other entities to achieve their self-causation.

Thus for Whitehead there is threefold causality:

1. Final causality—the process of self-causation;
2. Formal causation—flowing from the subjective aim—the mode whereby the entity acts and feels in self-causality;
3. Efficient causality, which is the past exercising on the present, the present on the future, is helping entities achieve their self-causation. Efficiency is an effect of finality.

There is no real material causality, since there is no substance. There is an analogous substitute—the wealth of objectified entities, data, etc., all of which are potentials for new becoming, for every entity which has arrived at satisfaction is a potential for every becoming.

The aim of all causality is the production of new actual entities, in the vast progressive flux postulated by the philosophy of organism.

CHAPTER V

GOD IN WHITEHEAD'S PHILOSOPHY

There is a necessary connection between metaphysics and theodicy. If any system of thought is metaphysical, it must deal with ultimate principles, and ultimately, with *the* principle. If metaphysics is a science of principles and causes, there must be a solid foundation—real as well as logical—upon which these principles rest and from which these principles depend. Hence, any metaphysical system truly such, must treat of God.

Whitehead claims that his philosophy is metaphysical, and he also claims that there is a place for God in his philosophy. He treats of God in many of his works, but especially in *Religion in the Making*, *Modes of Thought*, and *Process and Reality*, where the last section of the book is given over to a consideration of God in Whiteheadian philosophy. Whitehead further claims that his notion of God, differing greatly from the Christian notion, is entirely consistent with his philosophy, and completely in accord with his metaphysics.

> "In the first place, God is not to be treated as an exception to all metaphysical principles, invoked to save their collapse. He is their chief exemplification."[1]

In carrying this out, Whitehead seems to think that he is forced to depart from the accepted notions of God. He does so depart. Whether he is forced to do so or not is another question. Furthermore, by presupposing that he is correct in his concept of God, he is thereby implying that all other systems are incorrect, and should revise their philosophies to fit his.

Before going any further, we can say now that God is the test and transcendent exemplar of Whitehead's philosophical system, and that further in this system God is the projection of man's yearning for a personal God. In trying to reconcile those two approaches to God, we find a great deal of confusion that is difficult to understand and disentangle. In following out this investigation of Whitehead's theodicy, we shall consider: (i) Whitehead's evaluation of the accepted notions of God; (ii) Whitehead's proofs for the existence of God; (iii) Whitehead's explanation of the nature of God.

---
[1] *Process and Reality*, p. 521.

Whitehead's Evaluation of Traditional and Philosophical Notions of God

Whitehead is professedly opposed to traditional philosophical notions of God. He is especially opposed to the Aristotelian (and Christian) doctrine of the 'unmoved mover' and to the Christian doctrine of God as being 'eminently real.' Later on we shall see that he is opposed to God as 'pure act.' Concerning the first two notions, he says:

> "The notion of God as the 'unmoved mover' is derived from Aristotle, at least so far as Western thought is concerned. The notion of God as 'eminently real' is a favourite doctrine of Christian theology. The combination of the two into the doctrine of an aboriginal, eminently real, transcendent creator, at whose fiat the world came into being, and whose imposed will it obeys, is the fallacy which has infused tragedy into the histories of Christianity and of Mahometanism."[2]

Whitehead tries to give an historical attempt to reject those notions when he says:

> "When the Western world accepted Christianity, Caesar conquered; and the received text of Western theology was edited by its lawyers. The code of Justinian and the theology of Justinian are two volumes expressing one movement of the human spirit. The brief Galilean vision of humility flickered throughout the ages, uncertainly. In the official formulation of the religion it has assumed the trivial form of the mere attribution to the Jews that they cherished a misconception about their Messiah. But the deeper idolatry of the fashioning of God in the image of the Egyptian, Persian, and Roman imperial rulers was retained. The Church gave unto God the attributes which belonged exclusively to Caesar."[3]

Whitehead also inveighs against the merging of Christianity, in its tendency to consider God as an imperial ruler, with Mohammedan doctrine of God the image of an imperial ruler, the image and personification of moral energy, the image of an ultimate philosophical principle. Also of all men to claim as a champion in exploding these beliefs, he cites David Hume in his *Dialogues*.

In opposition to these philosophical and theological considerations of God, Whitehead appeals to the Christian notion of love,

---
[2] *Process and Reality*, p. 519.
[3] *Ibid.*, pp. 519, 520.

and it is here, I believe, that he projects man's yearning for a personal God into the argument for his own explanation of God. He says:

> "There is, however, in the Galilean origin of Christianity yet another suggestion which does not fit very well with any of the three main strands of thought. It does not emphasize the ruling Caesar, or the ruthless moralist, or the unmoved mover. It dwells upon the tender elements in the world, which slowly and in quietness operate by love; and it finds purpose in the present immediacy of a kingdom not of this world. Love neither rules, nor is it unmoved; also it is a little oblivious as to morals. It does not look to the future; for it finds its own reward to the immediate present."[4]

Thus, then, Whitehead rejects the notion of God as an imperial ruler, as a ruthless moralist, and as an ultimate philosophical principle. He does this, I think, because he wishes to preserve the notion of a kindly, provident, loving God. He seems to consider God the imperial ruler as an abstract absentee landlord, God the moralist as a ruthless, Puritanical spirit of vengeance, and God the philosophical principle as an abstract unmoved mover in whom is no providence. Whitehead's explanation of the nature of God will be an attempt to reconcile God as the chief exemplar of philosophy of organism, with the Galilean spirit of love. Without here and now going into the question of whether or not Whitehead is correct in his conclusions and in his premises, especially those from history, we shall pass on to his proofs for the existence of God.

WHITEHEAD'S PROOFS FOR THE EXISTENCE OF GOD

Whitehead does not have any special place in his philosophical works to prove the existence of God. These proofs are implicit in his system. He does not spend much time concerning the proofs for God's existence. His position seems to be that God's existence in the terms which Whitehead understands Him is obvious from the nature of the philosophy of organism, and a proof would be superfluous. He rather spends his time in trying to shape out his notion of God's nature, in trying to come to a harmonious agreement of all the post-Cartesian notions of God as advanced by non-Scholastic philosophers.

---
[4] *Ibid.*, p. 520.

However, in many places in Whitehead's works, the premises for proofs for God's existence are given, and it is upon these that we must build up what seem to be Whitehead's proofs. Here we are indebted to Dr. Charles Hartshorne of the University of Chicago.[5] Dr. Hartshorne is not a scholastic, and in many respects is in close agreement with Whitehead. However, he has done the valuable work of going through Whitehead's many writings and formulating the grounds from which we should deduce the existence of God in Whitehead's philosophy. Again, I must repeat, that the God deduced from these Whitehead principles is not the God of Christian revelation.

Dr. Hartshorne reduces Whitehead's proofs to six, which I think can be reduced to five, and ultimately, to three, which are:

1. From contingent things to a necessary being, that is not necessary in every respect;

2. From formality ordained to finality in each actual event; based on an intuitive recognition of order, leading to a God who is the principle of concrescence, who instills this intuitive sense of order;

3. From a graded participation in existence to God who is dynamic existence, living a life of self-perfecting.

The five proofs which we will investigate are:

1. From contingency;
2. From participation of all things in existence;
3. From cosmological order to a supreme ordering factor, a supreme principle of concrescence;
4. From memory—i.e., from the memory of duration underlying change to an active principle of active duration;
5. From teleology—i.e., the supreme principle of concretion is the End, the Good, as well as the formal principle of all things. Throughout all these proofs, God is considered as the supreme example of Whiteheadian categories.

We might note that these proofs for God's Existence seem to be reducible to the fundamental principle of Whitehead's Philosophy, —the 'Ontological Principle'—namely, that in all reality, we have actuality and possibility, i.e., act and potency. The great reality is act, which, of course, Whitehead interprets as constant change.

---

[5] Hartshorne, Charles: *Whitehead's Idea of God*, in the anthology, *The Philosophy of Alfred North Whitehead*, p. 515 ff.

Whitehead's 'Ontological Principle' is formulated in several ways throughout his writings, but in respect to his theodicy it amounts to this, that possibility has no meaning without actuality; that possibility is ordained to actuality; that there can be no possibility without actuality.

However, the 'Ontological Principle' is not used to prove God's existence directly. It is used to prove creativity and becoming, to prove the unity in a dynamic universe, of which God is an accident,[6] or a necessary property. The 'Ontological Principle' proves the fact that things change, that they must come from some preexisting changing things, that they must be formed according to the 'eternal objects', and that God is necessary, not as a creator, but merely as a sustainer and director and guide of process.

The arguments run as follows:

1. *From Possibility.* There is a section in *Process and Reality* wherein Whitehead gives the basic postulates for his philosophy of organism. This section is Chapter I, entitled *Fact and Form* (pp. 63-94). In it, Whitehead says:

> "It is a contradiction in terms to assume that some explanatory fact can float into the actual world out of nonentity. Nonentity is nothingness. . . . The notion of 'subsistence' is merely the notion of how eternal objects can be components of the primordial nature of God."[7]

In other words, from nothing, nothing becomes, and subsistence depends upon the presence of forms in the mind of God. Things are constantly changing, constantly becoming either more or less perfect in themselves, or new things altogether. There is a great deal of process, and hence potentiality in the universe. But potentiality indicates a lack of due perfection, and hence, in relation to the due perfection yet to be achieved, potentiality is relatively nothing. In itself, it is an actual entity lacking a perfection. In relation to the perfection, it is a negation, and hence, a relative nothing. But, from nothing, nothing becomes, and so behind all the potentaility in the universe, there must be all-pervading actuality. Behind all this contingency, there must be something, to a certain extent, absolute. Note I say to a certain

---

[6] *Process and Reality*, p. 10.
[7] *Ibid.*, p. 73.

extent. Whitehead denies this principle's being absolute in every respect.

Now, for the actualization of this potentiality, for the notion of subsistence, God's primordial nature is required, for all actualization, all subsistence, all action is the mutual ingression of form and event, and God's primordial nature is presupposed for that.

That Whitehead would view potentiality from the notion of relative nothing is apparent not only from his written philosophy, but also from his training as a physicist. He looks upon change from the point of view of dynamic physics, and hence, would look upon potentiality in terms of potential energy. Potential energy, as we know, is opposed to kinetic energy. Kinetic energy is the actual operation of force. As the physicist would say, it is energy at work. Potential energy is energy which is not at work, but which is capable of operating. For example, a suspended weight is potential energy. It is not at work. It is doing nothing, expending no energy. There is no actual energy, and from the point of view of the dynamist, there is nothing.

Coming back again to this proof, we see that although Whitehead argues from contingency, he does not arrive at God as an absolutely necessary being. He arrives at God as a concomitant principle of process. He merely proves the fact that process is based upon activity. God is part of that activity, namely the principle of uniting change to form. It may be summed up in Whitehead's own words:

> "By this recognition of the divine element the general Aristotelian principle is maintained that, apart from things that are actual, there is nothing—nothing either in fact or in efficacy. This is the true general principle which also underlies Descartes' dictum: 'For this reason, when we perceive any attribute, we therefore conclude that some existing thing or substance to which it may be attributed, is necessarily present.' And again: 'For every clear and distinct conception (*perceptio*) is without doubt something and hence cannot derive its origin from what is nought. . .' This general principle will be termed the 'ontological principle.' It is the principle that everything is positively somewhere in actuality, and in potency everywhere."[8]

Hence, this argument from contingency does not prove the exist-

---

[8] *Process and Reality*, p. 64.

ence of God. It only proves the necessity of actuality, and in doing so, presupposes the existence of God, and of a God far different from the commonly accepted notion.

2. *From Participation in Existence.* Professor Whitehead's philosophical hero seems to be Plato. He claims to be a Platonist, and he maintains that the great philosopher of the West is Plato. He says, "The safest general characterization of the European philosophical tradition is that it consists of a series of footnotes to Plato. I do not mean the systematic scheme of thought which scholars have doubtfully extracted from his writings. I allude to the wealth of general ideas scattered through them."[9] If Whitehead is a Platonist, he should have a doctrine of participation, for that is a fundamentally Platonic doctrine. In Plato, we find it developed in the *Phaedo, Philebus, Republic. Timaeus,* and *Symposium.* The argument as developed by Plato is, briefly, that if things participate to a greater or lesser degree in Love, there must be a fullness of Love in which they participate. And that Love is God. The argument is valid if the objective participation is proved. If the participation is not proved, then the argument supposes what it is intended to prove. In its valid form, we recognize St. Thomas's fourth proof for the existence of God.

Let us see what Whitehead has to say on participation. We must remember that he claims to be a Platonist. We can say that Whitehead bases his whole philosophy upon participation.

> "In such a philosophy the actualities constituting the process of the world are conceived as exemplifying the ingression (or 'participation') of other things which constitute the potentialities of definiteness for any actual existence. The things which are temporal arise by their participation in the things which are eternal. The two sets are mediated by a thing which combines the actuality of what is temporal with the timelessness of what is potential. This final entity is the divine element in the world, by which the barren inefficient disjunction of abstract potentialities obtains primordially the efficient conjunction of ideal realization."[10]

This is developed in two ways by Whitehead. In *Process and Reality,* he makes use of it as the basis of organism. Entities are constantly gaining perfections. In doing so, they prehend, or feel

---
[9] *Process and Reality,* p. 63.
[10] *Ibid.,* p. 63. The parenthetical insertion is Whitehead's.

and accept the 'givenness' of other entities, and especially do they participate in 'eternal objects'—somewhat akin to what we call forms, or, in certain respects, qualities. Whitehead's own example is participation in a definite shade of green. The shade of green exists as an 'eternal object' because it is not limited to the entity which here and now displays it. Other objects may also display it even though they do not do so. However, all may potentially participate in it, even though only one object actuallty does participate in it. Thus, each occasion is 'ideally realized' by participation in various 'eternal objects'.

Note that this argument does not directly prove the existence of God. It simply proves participation in ideal forms. However, it postulates God, or the 'divine element,' because actual occasions (individual things) and 'eternal objects' "are mediated by a thing which combines the actuality of what is temporal with the timelessness of what is potential. This final entity is the divine element in the world . . ." As such the argument is not a univocal argument. It is rather hybrid, in as much as it states a fact that postulates the existence of God. It directly proves participation, and then postulates God as an agent to unite events into forms.

However, in *Modes of Thought,* Whitehead treats of participation in a more univocal manner. He shows that all things contain the one common denominator of existence. They all participate in existence. There is an awareness of existence, a social awareness of it that cannot come from the thing's awareness of its own existence only. Existence is a public fact, and there is the consciousness of it as a public or social fact. This, of course, is a necessary postulate in a relativistic philosophy.

When Whitehead speaks of the existence of any or all things, he speaks of their full existence, as they really are in all their completeness. Hence, for him, existence takes on a meaning of value, which the thing is in itself, and of value in which the thing may become. It means the thing fully in itself, and fully in all its relations, present and future.

In this, we must remember two factors, namely, that existence for Whitehead is dynamic insofar as existence is becoming, and that relations are considered in terms of sympathetic relations. And, if all things participate in existence which is becoming and which is relation, there must be a transcendently objective existence which is the Great Becoming and which is the transcendence of sympathy. This, of course, is God, who is, characteristically immanent in the world, but not transcendent in our understanding of the term. This notion of God as the Great Immanent Becoming, the great principle of sympathy, is the foundation, I think, of those attributes of tenderness with which Whitehead would endow God. But we must remember that for Whitehead, God is tenderly immanent in the world, but transcendent only inasmuch as He is the supreme example of Whitehead's categories.

3. *From Cosmological Order.* We have already seen something of this in the note of participation. We shall see more of it in considering the primordial and consequent natures of God. We have seen that in the philosophy of organism, process is largely the mutual ingression of ideal forms and individual events. There is a definite pattern of forms according to which this process advances, and God is the guardian and guide of those patterns.

> "In such a philosophy the actualities constituting the process of the world are conceived as exemplifying the ingression (or 'participation') of other things which constitute the potentialities of definiteness for any actual existence. The things which are temporal arise by their participation in the things which are eternal. The two sets are mediated by a thing which combines the actuality of what is temporal with the timelessness of what is potential. This final entity is the divine element in the world, by which the barren inefficient disjunction of abstract potentialities obtains primordially the efficient conjunction of ideal realization."[11]

In this particular citation we see that it is the 'divine element' that joins forms to individuals—or rather, causes forms to ingress into individuals. That would make God more an efficient cause than a formal cause.

In *Adventures of Ideas*, Whitehead writes about order in the world (Chapters VII and VIII). He speaks of it in terms of 'law' and gives four tentative explanations of the law of order. That is not so important as his scientific belief in order in the world. His approach is not so much that God is a formal cause, as that He is a final cause. As we saw in the investigation of causality in Whitehead's philosophy, all things get their initial phase from God, which seems equivalent to saying that God gives each thing its formal cause. By doing so, He extracts finality out of each

---

[11] *Process and Reality*, p. 63.

thing. He unites individuals to forms in order to gain harmony in the universe.

> "From this point of view, he (God) is the principle of concretion—the principle whereby there is initiated a definite outcome from a situation otherwise riddled with ambiguity."[12]

It is put more clearly in the last words of *Religion in the Making:*

> "The present type of order in the world has arisen from an unimaginable past, and it will find its grave in an unimaginable future. There remain the inexhaustible realm of abstract forms, and creativity, with its shifting character even determined a fresh by its own creatures, and God, upon whose wisdom all forms of order depend."[13]

These recognitions of cosmic order, on a large scale, as postulating the existence of the 'divine element' to guide process, come close to our proof for God's existence from design. However, Whitehead does not reach God distinct from the world, planning design and sustaining order by divine concurrence. He reaches God as part of the great process, extracting harmonious process out of all concrescence. And God perfects Himself in so guiding and so guarding. All the way through Whitehead's treatment of order, in the two chapters mentioned above in *Adventures of Ideas*, the note of God as immanent is the keynote stressed, since as Whitehead claims, it is a Platonic note. He claims that it flows from the definition of being as power, which Whitehead himself accepts.

> "It was Plato in his later mood who put forward the suggestion, 'and I hold that the definition of being is simply power.' This suggestion is the charter of the doctrine of Immanent Law."[14]

Whitehead constantly follows the theme of God being only immanent, and not separate (which we understand by 'transcendent') from the world.

4. *From Teleology.* Whitehead is credited with having introduced finality into non-Scholastic philosophy. Whether this is true or not is another question, but there is no doubt that finality plays a part of prime importance in the philosophy of organism. Whitehead's whole system is an effort to explain order in diversity, and to prove it by giving each actual occasion a definite role and a

---

[12] *Process and Reality*, p. 523. The parenthetical insertion is mine.
[13] *Religion in the Making*, p. 160.
[14] *Adventures of Ideas*, p. 165.

definite development which is in itself orderly, and which contributes to the great order of the universe. This notion of teleology reaches its culmination in God extracting harmony from the orderly sequence of each event, and it goes hand in hand with Whitehead's emphasis upon cosmic order. This emphasis upon teleology, especially with the notion of harmony, is to be found throughout the works of Whitehead, but is admirably summarized in the last section of *Religion in the Making*.

"God is that function in the world by reason of which our purposes are directed to ends which in our own consciousness are impartial as to our own interests. He is that element in life in virtue of which judgment stretches beyond facts of existence to values for ourselves to values for others. He is that element in virtue of which the attainment of such a value for others transforms itself into value for ourselves.

"He is the binding element in the world. The consciousness which is individual in us, is universal in him: the love which is partial in us is all-embracing in him ..."[15]

Note the connection between teleology and participation. God is the final cause of all things because he is the fullness of what is partial in individual entities. Whitehead is here bordering upon a profoundly metaphysical truth, namely, the intrinsic connection between participation in being and perfection and finality.

Whitehead states this connection between participation and finality in *Process and Reality* as follows:

"The things which are temporal arise by their participation in the things which are eternal. The two sets are mediated by a thing which combines the actuality of what is temporal with the timelessness of what is potential. This final entity is the divine element in the world, by which the barren inefficient disjunction of abstract potentialities obtains primordially the efficient conjunction of ideal realization. This ideal realization of potentialities in a primordial actual entity constitutes the metaphysical stability whereby the actual process exemplifies general principles of metaphysics and attains the ends proper to specific types of emergent order."[16]

That above citation, treating of the connection between participation and finality has more to do with God implanting the initial phase of each entity, namely, placing in it its tendency to a given

---
[15] *Religion in the Making*, p. 158.
[16] *Process and Reality*, p. 63.

end. It has to do with the interplay of finality and formality. But God not only implants a tendency to finality into each individual by implanting the initial aim, he also guides that aim by in His role as the great final cause of all process:

> "He is the lure for feeling, the eternal urge of desire. His particular relevance to each creative act as it arises from its own conditioned standpoint in the world, constitutes him the initial 'object of desire' establishing the initial phase of each subjective aim."[17]

Thus, in a way, God may be said to be the beginning and end of all things. He is the beginning of them by establishing their initial aim, the private ends towards which they tend. He is the end of them all since by His own attraction, He causes them to tend to their own particular ends, and ultimately to Himself. Moreover, in this process, He is their constant guardian and guide. This seems analogous to our notion of the divine concurrence, and is the reason why, at the beginning of this consideration of Whitehead's proofs for the existence of God, it was said that the argument from formality and the argument from finality could be reduced to one argument.

Yet again, this argument does not so much prove God's existence as presuppose it. After all, Whitehead lays great emphasis upon each entity tending towards the 'eternal objects' and seeking 'objective immortality.' To explain that he postulates God, his own peculiar notion of God. It comes close to saying that God proves finality and finality proves God.

5. *From Memory, or Everlastingness.* This argument may be summarized briefly. We all have a sense of duration. We feel that something remains amid change.

We have seen from the previous arguments that in the constant process which is the universe, there is constant finality according to definite, formal patterns. This is attested to by memory as well as proved by metaphysics. All of these, plus memory, lead to the conclusion that there is an everlasting principle which is in a certain sense temporal, and in another sense non-temporal.[18] If this constant process goes on eternally—and Whitehead holds that view—then the support and chief exemplification of this process must be eternal.

---

[17] *Ibid.*, p. 522.
[18] Cf. *Adventures of Ideas*, p. 267.

God in Whitehead's Philosophy 71

All these arguments, namely, from contingency, from participation, from cosmic order, from finality, and from a sense of everlastingness are arguments upon which Whitehead depends for the existence of God. They should be arguments for the existence of God, although some of them rather postulate God than prove His existence. Yet they lead us, according to Whitehead's development, into a notion of God that is far different than the traditional Christian notions of Him. We shall now take up Whitehead's notion of the nature of God.

WHITEHEAD'S NOTION OF THE NATURE OF GOD

In entering this consideration, it is necessary to note that the one doing so has to puzzle over a maze of terms and apparent contradictions. Whether these contradictions are only apparent remains to be seen. We might further note that one will not get much clarification from admirers of Whitehead, or, in general, from modern non-Scholastic philosophers. Such philosophers all have strange—and at times bizarre—notions of God. Furthermore, among Thomists, many able minds have undertaken a critique of Whitehead's notion of the nature of God. These men, too, have confessed the confusion that is rampant in Whitehead's theodicy, and have admitted their inability to reach definite certitude concerning Whitehead's views on the subject. Hence this treatment lays no claim to announce what Whitehead thinks or believes concerning God. It is an attempt to clarify what Whitehead writes on the subject.

Whitehead's ex professo treatment of God is to be found in the last chapter (*God and the World*) of *Process and Reality* (pp. 519-533). Some clarifications of the doctrine therein contained are to be found in *Religion in the Making*. Of the two, although the latter work is slightly more clear, the former is to be held as more authoritative, since Whitehead's theodicy has undergone successive changes in his successive works, and there is a definite change in *Process and Reality*, written after *Religion in the Making*, and representing, as far as we know, Whitehead's notions of God in philosophy. What he may hold as a religious man, we do not know.

In the proofs for the existence of God, we saw that all process, participation, contingency, formality, and finality of individual entities lead to an ultimate. As to the question, "What is the ultimate, God?" We have to answer in the negative. Whitehead has the following to say about the ultimate:

> "In all philosophic theory there is an ultimate which is actual in virtue of its accidents. It is only then capable of characterization through its accidental embodiments, and apart from these accidents is devoid of actuality. In the philosophy of organism, this ultimate is termed 'creativity'; and God is its primordial, non-temporal accident."[19]

Now, I do not think we should accuse Whitehead of things he does not mean to say. This can be easily done by our wrongly attacking him on the word 'accident.' The fault is his for using a term like 'accident' in a meaning far different from the long-accepted meaning of it, namely, as 'that which inheres in another as in a subject.' We can attack Whitehead on his use of the term, but not on our understanding of it, even though we know he is giving it a different meaning. For Whitehead, accident seems to mean 'that which gives actuality to potentiality.'

That God exists with creativity, to perfect Himself by putting creativity into act, seems to be born out by the rest of Whitehead's theodicy. We see this especially in his postulate of God's threefold characters, namely, his 'primordial nature,' 'consequent nature,' and 'superjective nature.' We find this stated as follows:

> "In the case of the primordial actual entity, which is God, there is no past. Thus the ideal realization of conceptual feeling takes the precedence. God differs from other actual entities in the fact that Hume's principle, of the derivate character of conceptual feelings does not hold for him. There is still, however, the same threefold character: (i) the 'primordial' nature of God is the concrescence of an unity of conceptual feelings, including among their data all eternal objects. The concrescence is is directed by the subjective aim, that the subjective forms of the feelings shall be such as to constitute the eternal objects into relevant lures of feeling severally appropriate for all realizable basic conditions. (ii) The 'consequent nature' of God is the physical prehension by God of the actualities of the evolving universe. This primordial nature directs such perspectives of objectification that each noval actuality in the temporal world contributes such elements as it can to a realization in God free from inhibitions of intensity by reason of discordance. (iii)

---

[19] *Process and Reality*, p. 10.

The 'superjective' nature of God is the character of the pragmatic value of his specific satisfaction qualifying the transcendent creativity in the various temporal instances."[20]

We must notice in this that God is the 'primordial actual entity,' *not* the ultimate principle. That means that God *is not* creativity. He shares in it, for every actual entity shares in creativity. This assertion, also, is borne out by a consideration, rather in detail, of God's threefold nature. It is thus that God is not an exception to metaphysics, but rather a supreme example of it. God too has his subjective aim, and God too goes through the change of process. God too follows creativity, and although He directs it in others, He follows it in His own life, since in directing it in others, He is by that very fact subject to it Himself. According to Whitehead's scheme, God is necessary for the world, but the world is also necessary for God.

"God is the infinite ground of all mentality, the unity of vision seeking physical multiplicity. The world is the multiplicity of finites, actualities seeking a perfected unity. Neither God nor the world reaches static completion. Both are in the grip of ultimate metaphysical ground, the creative advance into novelty. Either of them, God and the World, is the instrument of novelty for the other."[21]

The mutual dependence of God and the world upon each other we shall now see in a consideration of the threefold nature of God.

1. *The Primordial Nature of God.* This, I think, is one of the most difficult tenets of Whitehead's philosophy to understand. There are words, many words, used to describe and explain it, but the meaning of those words is another question. And, they are going to lead into subjectivism. Whitehead tells us that "any cogency of argument entirely depends upon elucidation of somewhat exceptional elements in our conscious experience—those elements which may roughly be classed together as religious and moral intuitions."[22] The history of the human race has shown that religion and morality must be objective to be followed subjectively. Intuitional religion and morality have led into many aberrations of doctrine and practice. Hence, dependence upon "religious and

---

[20] *Process and Reality*, p. 134.
[21] *Ibid.*, p. 529.
[22] *Ibid.*, p. 521.

moral intuition" to clarify philosophical tenets will scarcely lead to unity of thought,—save when it refers to first principles of being and acting.

The primordial nature of God is described as follows:

> "Viewed as primordial, he is the unlimited conceptual realization of the absolute wealth of potentiality. In this aspect, he is not *before* all creation, but *with* creation."[23]

The most obvious meaning therein expressed is that God is the great attraction for all things from the very beginning of them and yet is within the entire process of reality, in fact even while they are only possibilities. They find in Him their satisfaction, and apparently both He and they exist only conceptually.

> "But, as primordial, so far is he from 'eminent reality,' that in this abstraction he is 'deficiently actual'—and this in two ways. His feelings are only conceptual and so lack the fulness of actuality. Secondly, conceptual feelings, apart from complex integration with physical feelings, are devoid of consciousness in their subjective forms."[24]

Now, apparently, this means the following:

(a) In all things there is an innate, unconscious, tendancy towards unity and towards enrichment in value. (". . . conceptual feelings, apart from complex integration with physical feelings, are devoid of consciousness in their subjective forms.")

(b) This harmony in tendency and value postulates God as its organizer, the locust of the eternal objects which ingress into actual entities.

> "From this point of view, he (God) is the principle of concretion—the principle whereby there is initiated a definite outcome from a situation otherwise riddled with ambiguity."[25]

> "The present type of order in the world has arisen from an unimaginable past, and it will find its grave in an unimaginable future. There remain the inexhaustible realm of abstract forms, and creativity, with its shifting character ever determined afresh by its own creatures, and God, upon whose wisdom all forms of order depend."[26]

---

[23] *Process and Reality*, p. 521.
[24] *Ibid.*, p. 521.
[25] *Ibid.*, p. 525. The parenthetical insertion is mine.
[26] *Religion in the Making*, p. 160; Cf. *Process and Reality*, p. 73.

And, note what has been said above in the proof for God's existence from formality and finality.

(c) God exists in his primordial nature only conceptually as the value phase in these conceptual feelings as the initial object of desire—and thus each entity may be said to derive its initial aim from God, not only in the sense that God implants the initial aim into them, but also in the sense that in their initial aim, they tend towards realization in God. He is thus not before creation, but with creation, since His own undeveloped conceptual feelings depend upon the conceptual feelings of actual occasions tending to him as a principle of harmony. Again, the ultimate principle is not God, but creativity, of which God is an accident.

We might even go so far as to say that God is the initial desire. "He is unconditioned actuality of conceptual feeling at the base of things; so that, by reason of this primordial actuality, there is an order in the relevance of eternal objects to the process of creation. . . . The primordial nature of God is the acquirement by creativity of a primordial character."[27] That would seem to say that God exists the great final cause in which all things reach their idealization. In fact, Whitehead says that "He is the presupposed actuality of conceptual operation, in unison of becoming with every other creative act."[28] If, as Whitehead seems to maintain, creativity and creation are eternal, then God, as this final cause, is eternal, and His eternity is based upon His primordial nature as the eternal final cause, the wealth of potentialities, the fact that all things are realizable in him. In this sense, He is conceptual.

2. *God's Consequent Nature.* In keeping with the above, especially in view of Whitehead's postulate that God starts out "deficient in actuality," and also in view of the fact that God gains actuality by actual occasions being realized in him, Whitehead postulates God's consequent nature. This is the other pole in God's dipolarity. On the one hand, God, as primordial, is the wealth of conceptualism. God as consequent is actuality.

> "But God, as well as being primordial, is also consequent. He is the beginning and the end. He is not the beginning in the sense of being in the past of all members. He is the presupposed actuality of conceptual operation, in unison of becoming with every other creative act.

---

[27] *Process and Reality*, p. 522.
[28] *Ibid.*, p. 522.

> Thus by reason of the relativity of all things, there is a reaction of the world on God. The completion of God's nature into a fulness of physical feeling is derived from the objectification of the world in God. He shares with every new creation its actual world; and the concrescent creature is objectified in God as a novel element in God's objectification of that actual world. This prehension into God of each creature is directed with the subjective aim, and clothed with the subjective form, wholly derivative from his all inclusive primordial valuation. God's conceptual nature is unchanged, by reason of its final completeness. But his derivative nature is consequent upon the creative advance of the world."[29]

Or again:

> "The consequent nature of God is the fulfillment of his experience by his reception of the multiple freedom of actuality into the harmony of his own actualization. It is God as really actual, completing the deficiency of his mere conceptual actuality."[30]

Briefly, it amounts to this. In God's primordial nature, He is conceptual, and is deficient in actuality, and actual in deficiency as the final cause of all things. But, at any rate, He is deficient. In his consequent nature, He guides all things to their own individual and particular ends. Furthermore, in doing so, He carefully blends all these particular and individual processes into a harmony by guiding them to the reaching of 'objective immortality,' which seems to be the reaching of God as their final cause. In that harmonious process, He himself acquires actuality, and thus is enriched. Where, in His primordial nature He was merely conceptual, the standard of valuation,—but yet real,—now, in His consequent nature, He is physically actual. In His primordial nature He was ideally actual. Now He is physically actual. Thus, God's role as primordial is reality as a valuation of all possibilities. His role as consequent is reality as process. In His consequent nature, in drawing harmony out of apparent disunity, He "reaches from end to end and orders all things sweetly"—not by physical coercion.

> "If we conceive the first term and the last term in their unity over against the intermediate multiple freedom of physical realizations in the temporal world, we conceive

---
[29] *Process and Reality*, p. 529.
[30] *Ibid.*, p. 530.

of the patience of God, tenderly saving the turmoil of the intermediate world by the completion of his own nature. The sheer force of things lies in the intermediate physical process: this is the energy of physical production. God's role is not the combat of productive force with productive force, of destructive force with destructive force: it lies in the patient operation of the overpowering rationality of his conceptual harmonization. He does not create the world, he saves it: or, more accurately, he is the poet of the world, with tender patience leading it by his vision of truth, beauty, goodness."

"The consequent nature of God is his judgment on the world. He saves the world as it passes into the immediacy of his own life. It is the judgment of a tenderness which loses nothing that can be saved. It is also the judgment of a wisdom which uses what in the temporal world is mere wreckage."[31]

This contrast between God's primordial nature and his consequent nature is best brought out by a consideration of—

3. *God's Dipolarity.* This is a contrast between the two natures to show how they complete one another.

God's Primordial Nature	*God's Consequent Nature*
Conceptual—the infinite valuation of all entities; conceptual in himself, and the conceived final cause in all entities.	Conscious realization of the actual world in unity of nature through transformation of God's wisdom in ordering things, by weaving in primordial concepts.
As the wealth of possibilities, infinite; free, complete, eternal —because the wealth of possibilities is infinite, and God's primordial nature is the measure of these, hence infinite and eternal; actually deficient, unconscious.	From physical experience derived from the ingression of the temporal world being realized in God; determined,[32] incomplete, 'everlasting,' fully actual, conscious, finite.
Originating in conceptual experience.	Completing the conceptual process of both God and actual entities; realizing final causes.
Value of conceptual experience in actual entities in their initial phase.	Derived from the process of actual entities into God via 'objective immortality.'

---

[31] *Process and Reality*, p. 525.
[32] *Religion in the Making*, p. 150: "To be an actual thing is to be imited."

God's Primordial Nature	God's Consequent Nature
The everlasting and infinite standard of values *for* the world.[33]	The world becomes everlasting *in* God.[33]
Conceptually infinite.	Actually finite.

Mention has been made of Whitehead's projection of man's yearnings for a personal, sympathetic God. This plays its part in order through formality and finality. To review a bit. The approach to God is by an interplay of formality and finality. In the world we see constant process, constant change, constant beginnings and annihilations. Now, as we learn from human experience, there could be a great deal of frustration and mutual destruction in all this. There could be vast chaos. Yet, on the contrary, there is, on the whole, a wonderful order in each thing. Each thing exists to serve its purpose. Whereas the energy that pervades each individual thing could run amuck and raise havoc, it does not do so. Instead, it causes order and well-being. This is, again, Whitehead's doctrine of 'immanent law.' This is God's 'primordial nature,' God as the 'value phase.' To repeat a citation:

"God is that function in the world by reason of which our purposes are directed to ends which in our own consciousness are impartial to our own interests. . . ."[34]

Furthermore, besides individual order, there is mutual and social order. After all, what we call chance is not lack of order and finality. It is based upon each thing's acting according to its end. To offset it, or to prevent it in a large scale, there is social order, order among, as well as in, entities. God is the principle of all that order, as seen above in the proof for God's existence from order and design.

And what is most wonderful is that there is order in spite of and drawn from frustration. There is frustration in the world. That is too obvious to be ignored. What is amazing is that frustration itself serves a higher order. For example, when minerals are absorbed by plant roots, they lose their individuality in destruction. But in so being destroyed, they are drawn into and made part of a much higher order of association, namely, life. When grass is

---

[33] *Process and Reality*, p. 527.
[34] *Religion in the Making*, p. 158.

eaten by cattle, the grass is frustrated, and yet by that fact, made part of the order of sensitive life. When the cattle is killed and eaten by man, in the frustration thereby ensued, it becomes a part of a still higher order. When American soldiers were killed in war, their frustration was a sacrifice for the attainment of ideals to be attained (we hope) in a better post-war world. And thus, constantly, harmony is drawn from frustration and destruction. This is the full application of all that Whitehead writes about 'eternal objects' and 'immanent law'.

This note of finality and formality drawn from evil is the special approach to a personal God on the part of Whitehead. He does not stop at arguing from individual formality and finality, from social interaction of formality and finality, to a principle of intelligence. He does not let go at that, as did Aristotle, who built up the notion of God the first immovable mover from eternal motion, and who ended up with God as a principle of finality and as an 'absentee landlord.' Whitehead tries to argue to a personal God by postulating a principle that extracts good out of evil. His ultimate, the principle of process, goes on endlessly and ruthlessly. In its advance, all the noble elements of the world perish. To save these values, to preserve them, to prevent the waste of them, a kindly, providential God is postulated. Whitehead grows lyrical about God in this aspect. He speaks of His spirit of "tenderness" and calls Him "the poet of the world." His being the 'value phase' of each entity, guiding them by attraction to individual and social order of finality and formality, is His 'primordial nature.' (Vide supra.) His operation in the achievement of individual value and social value in spite of and out of frustration, is His 'consequent nature.' To put it in his words:

> "The consequent nature of God is his judgment on the world. He saves the world as it passes into the immediacy of his own life. It is the judgment of a tenderness which loses nothing that can be saved. It is also the judgment of a wisdom which uses what in the temporal world is mere wreckage."[35]

The entire process is further described in a continuation of the same quotation:

> "Another image which is also required to understand his

---

[35] *Process and Reality*, p. 525.

consequent nature, is that of his infinite patience. The universe includes a threefold creative act composed of (i) the one infinite conceptual realization, (ii) the multiple solidarity of free physical realizations in the temporal world, (iii) the ultimate unity of the multiplicity of actual fact with the primordial conceptual fact. If we conceive the first term and the last term in their unity over against the intermediate multiple freedom of physical realizations in the temporal world, we conceive of the patience of God, tenderly saving the turmoil of the intermediate world by the completion of his own nature. The sheer force of things lies in the intermediate physical process: this is the energy of physical production. God's role is not the combat of productive force with productive force, of destructive force with destructive force; it lies in the patient operation of the over-powering rationality of his conceptual harmonization. He does not create the world, he saves it: or, more accurately, he is the poet of the world, with tender patience leading it by his vision of truth, beauty, and goodness."[36]

In this cosmic process, then, God exercises no physical power. He directs things through the quest for value. He is enriched by the achievement of value on the part of things, for they then enrich his own nature by making that value that had been conceptual now 'eminently real.' They are both part of the same process. The world needs God, and God needs the world, both requiring each other for their enrichment in process.

"Opposed elements stand to each other in mutual requirement. In their unity they inhibit or contrast. God and the World stand to each other in this opposed requirement. God is the infinite ground of all mentality, the unity of vision seeking physical multiplicity. The world is the multiplicity of finites, actualities, seeking a perfected unity. Neither God, nor the world, reaches static completion. Both are in the grip of the ultimate metaphysical ground, the creative advance into novelty. Either of them, God and the World, is the instrument of novelty for the other."[37]

It may be easily seen that God is not infinite in the traditionally accepted notion of that term. If God, too, progresses; if He is enriched physically, even though He does guide the struggle against chaos and frustration, He is limited, and hence, *with*

---
[36] *Process and Reality*, p. 535.
[37] *Ibid.*, p. 529.

limits, and not infinite, which means *without* limits. Whitehead tells us this in so many words:

> "The limitation of God is his goodness. He gains his depth of actuality by his harmony of valuation. It is not true that God is in all respects infinite. If he were he would be evil as well as good. Also this unlimited fusion of evil with good would mean mere nothingness. He is something decided and is thereby limited."[38]

But now, what is the end and finale of all this mutual enrichment in the 'creative advance into novelty?' Does the process go on endlessly? Does it come to a static conclusion? What is the outcome?

Whitehead describes this in what he calls the "superjective' nature of God. This 'superjective' nature of God has been described earlier in *Process and Reality* thus:

> "The 'superjective' nature of God is the character of the pragmatic value of his specific satisfaction qualifying the transcendent creativity in the various temporal instances."[39]

Concerning the 'consequent' nature of God, he has said:

> "Each actuality in the temporal world has its reception into God's nature. The corresponding element in God's nature is not temporal actuality, but is the transmutation of that temporal actuality into a living, ever-present fact. An enduring personality in the temporal world is a route of occasions in which the successors with some peculiar completeness sum up their predecessors. The correlate fact in God's nature is an even more complete unity of life in a chain of elements for which succession does not mean loss of immediate unison. This element in God's nature inherits from the temporal counterpart according to the same principle as in the temporal world the future inherits from the past. Thus in the sense in which the present occasion is the person *now*, and yet with his own past, so the counterpart in God is that person in God."[40]

"That person in God" is Whitehead's notion of the kingdom of heaven. But note how different it is from the traditional notion of heaven. The traditional notion of heaven is of a person, distinct from God, being in the presence of God in order to see,

---
[38] *Religion in the Making*, p. 153.
[39] *Process and Reality.*, p. 134.
[40] *Ibid.*, p. 531.

love, and praise God. His notion is the Spinozan notion of absorption into God's nature. Whereas Spinoza's notion was static, this notion is dynamic. Furthermore, the kingdom of heaven is a function of God.

> "Thus the consequent nature of God is composed of a multiplicity of elements with individual self-realization. It is just as much a multiplicity as it is a unity; it is just as much one immediate fact as it is an unresting advance beyond itself. Thus the actuality of God must also be understood as a multiplicity of actual components in process of creation. This is God in his function of the kingdom of heaven."[41]

We might say that Whitehead's notions of the 'primordial' and 'consequent' natures of God are a concise summary of his entire philosophy. Each actual entity acts according to its active nature, causes itself, tends towards its subjective aim. This subjective aim is the value phase for each entity, and each entity tending towards its value does so as an individual and as a member of an organic totum which is the world. The value phases is the 'primordial' nature of God. God's 'primordial' nature exists conceptually as the 'lure for feeling.' The achievement of perfection in the ordered activity constitutes the 'consequent' nature of God, which is his function as the kingdom of heaven.

And now, back to our question at hand. What is the final outcome of it all? Does it stop or does it go on forever? According to Whitehead, it goes on forever, for the process repeats over and over again.

> "But the principle of universal relativity is not to be stopped at the consequent nature of God. This nature itself passes into the temporal world according to its gradation of relevance to the various concrescent occasions. There are thus four creative phases in which the universe accomplishes its actuality. There is first the phase of conceptual origination, deficient in actuality, but infinite in its adjustment of valuation. Secondly, there is the temporal phases of physical origination, with its multiplicity of actualities. In this phase full actuality is attained; but there is deficiency in the solidarity of individuals with each other. This phase derives its determinate conditions from the first phase. Thirdly, there is the phase of perfected actuality, in which the

---

[41] *Ibid.*, p. 531.

many are one everlastingly, without the qualification of any loss either of individual identity or of completeness of unity. In everlastingness, immediacy is reconciled with objective immortality. This phase derives the conditions of its being from the two antecedent phases. In the fourth phase, the creative action completes itself. For the perfected actuality passes back into the temporal world, and qualifies this world so that each temporal actuality includes it as an immediate fact of relevant experience. For the kingdom of heaven is with us today. The action of the fourth phase is the love of God for the world. It is the particular providence for particular occasions. What is done in the world is transformed into a reality in heaven, and the reality in heaven passes back into the world. By reason of this reciprocal relation, the love in the world passes into the love in heaven, and floods back again into the world. In this sense, God is the great companion—the fellow-sufferer who understands."[43]

Undoubtedly, this is a summary of the philosophy of organism. Process goes on endlessly, in the multitudes of actual entities which are born, live, and die as drops of experience, in the value phase, God, who directs, enriches, is enriched, and preserves all the good wrought in the process. Since God, too, progresses in the process, since He, too, is enriched—although endlessly,—He is the "great companion—the fellow-sufferer who understands." What a projection for man's yearning for a personal God! And yet, how far from the Christian theology of Redemption! How close, in some respects to Christianity! And yet, how far away!

As William Ernest Hocking explains in his excellent book *Science and the Idea of God,* Professor Whitehead has shown us that science cannot exclude the notion of God, but in itself it cannot explain it. We might summarize Whitehead's whole philosophy as well as his theodicy in the following words of Professor Hocking:

"His vision of the transformation of the physical by the realization of qualities waiting to be born, as if Plato's eternal ideas abandoned their impassivity and at the touch of divine persuasion entered the world of change and addressed themselves to our suffrages—this is Whitehead's poem and the valid message of his philosophy."[44]

---

[43] *Process and Reality,* p. 532.
[44] Hocking, Wm. E., *Science and the Idea of God,* p. 109.

God in Whitehead's Philosophy

I. *Whitehead's notion of God.* God is not (i) the imperial ruler, (ii) the ruthless moralist, (iii) the ultimate philosophical principle that Aristotelianism, Christianity, and Mohammedanism would make Him. Instead, He is tenderness and love.

II. *The Place of God in Whitehead's philosophy.* God is necessary:
  1. As the test and transcendent exemplar of Whitehead's philosophical system;
  2. As the projection of man's yearning for a personal God.

III. *Proofs for the Existence of God.*
  1. From contingency to a necessary being Who is not necessary in every respect.
  2. From graded participation of all things in existence;
  3. From cosmological order to a supreme ordering factor—a supreme principle of concrescence;
  4. From memory—i. e., from the memory of duration underlying change to an active principle of active duration.
  5. From teleology—i. e., the supreme principle of concrescence is the end, the good, as well as the formal principle of all things.
  N. B. Throughout these proofs, God is considered as the supreme example of Whiteheadian categories.

IV. *The Nature of God.* God is the great becoming, the source, principle of concrescence, and the end of all actual events. As the principle of process, He is by His very nature perfectable. There is a twofold nature in God:
  1. *God's Antecedent Nature*—God as the source of all possibilities, granting each event its initial phase, not before creation but with creation. God containing all possibilities of physical values conceptually. God as self-perfectable.
  2. *God's Consequent Nature*—God as the principle of concrescence and formality; God actually completing Himself in creation and concursus.
  3. The entire process goes on endlessly, preserving the good wrought, and keeping the *kingdom of heaven* with us now and forever. God is the "Great Companion—the fellow-sufferer who understands."

PART TWO

CRITIQUE OF WHITEHEAD'S PHILOSOPHY

FOREWORD

Before actually giving a critical consideration of the philosophy of Whitehead step by step, I think it would be better to give a few principles concerning the method and content matter of this criticism.

First, concerning the method, we may say that it is of primary importance, in criticizing the philosophy of organism, to thereby justify the system of Thomism. Thomism has been tried and found true. If it be objected that Thomism has been tried and found wanting, we may answer, as would Chesterton, that for those who have found it wanting, they have never tried it.

As for the actual manner of consideration, we have noted that in Whitehead's philosophy, he began with his notion of becoming and his principle of eternal change specified accordingly by eternal objects and worked up to his philosophy of God as the summation of his entire system. Hence, as we saw, Whitehead's philosophy of God repeats all that he had postulated before. Our consideration will follow the same pattern. After an investigation as to the validity of Whitehead's theory of knowledge by way of introduction, we shall consider (i) the Thomistic notion of being and becoming; (ii) the Thomistic notion of cause; (iii) the Thomistic philosophy of God, which is the summation of all the rest of St. Thomas's philosophy. In doing this, we shall contrast the philosophy of St. Thomas with the counterpart in the system of Whitehead.

Secondly, as to the content. If there is one thing that has been proven metaphysically, as well as empirically in history of philosophy, it is that any philosophy is going to hinge around two factors: (i) the nature of being as it exists outside of the mind, and (ii) the mental equipment with which man studies objective being or objective things. If we wish to maintain any learning or any science at all, we must admit that. We study things, and not simply ideas. If we deny either the existence of things or the power of the mind to know things as they are, then we must be logically sceptics and hold the position that no knowledge is possible. Hence, in order to guarantee the truth of knowledge, we must hold that (i) things are, in their very natures, knowable, and that (ii) the mind can know them. True, we admit that there are modifications on those two poles of knowledge, namely, things and the ability of the mind to know things. Some things are difficult to understand in themselves, because they are too vast to be known or grasped completely by the mind, or that they are too obscure to offer much data to the mind. Also, in our knowing of things, we must admit that the mind often colors the data of things because of its own subjective dispositions, for example, because of the interference of some of the mental faculties in the field of the intellect ('wishful thinking'), or because of lack of proper training. Yet, we must hold that concerning certain fundamental principles, the mind can attain with certitude to the nature of things. We must hold that, or else, all attempts at learning are vain.

A philosophy is built, then, upon two solid foundations: the fact that things are knowable, and the fact that the human mind can know them. Since these are the two supports, they are also the two points of weakness in any philosophy, and the two focal points of attack in a philosophical system. They are going to be the two sources of possible error in any philosophy. And yet of these two, the great possible source of error is going to be the approach of the human mind to the investigation of reality. The being, becoming, or being-and-becoming of the world outside of the mind is going to remain in the same definite patterns whether or not the individual mind knows it, for, despite the idealists (and here we have Whitehead on our side) the mind is not the cause of the objective world. Rather, the objective world in its knowability is the cause of our knowledge. If that definiteness in the pattern of the world is not true, then all knowledge is in vain, and history is the greatest deception yet known to man.

Hence, in the following criticism of Whitehead's philosophy, we shall undertake an investigation of his system of knowledge, since that is his approach to the external world and the equipment with which he understands reality; and an investigation of his interpretation of reality.

One last word before passing on to the Thomistic system of knowledge as compared to Whitehead's: we must take for granted what we shall attempt to prove later, namely, the Thomistic notion of being and substance. Whitehead denies both, and we must prove both. But we must suppose both until we prove them later on in the investigation of the Thomistic notion of being and becoming.

Let us suppose, then, for the time being, the following considerations: there is being and becoming in the world. Reality is one and reality is many. Things are and things change. All that we know from experience. We also know that throughout all of reality, in each thing (save God), there is a determining element and a determinable element. Things exist independently, and yet they depend upon causes and components in order that they may exist independently. The Thomistic answer to all of these problems is to reduce them to the basic problem of the One and the Many, Being and Becoming, and to explain them through potency and act. The Thomistic answer is as follows:
1. God—Pure Act, the Absolute Fulness of Being:
2. Creatures—a composition of potency (capacity) and act (the actual fulness of that capacity).
   Further subdivisions of potency and act:

	Potency	*Act*
In every created substance	Essence	Existence
In every created substance	Substance	Accidents
In created corporeal substances	Matter	Form

Furthermore, our notion of substance is not that of an inert substratum, or 'that which exists by itself.' Our notion of substance is 'that which is apt to exist in its own right,' and 'principle of identity within the thing.' Our notion of substance is an active notion. If substance were not active, there would be no activity.

Lastly, our notion of being is active, not static. The same may be said of God, for He is a substance. Nor is each created thing dwelling in what Whitehead calls 'awful independence' of the rest of the universe. We, too, as much as and perhaps more than Whitehead, believe that each thing exists in a close dependence and interdependence with the rest of the universe. The whole universe depends directly as well as ultimately upon God, Who Alone is absolutely Independent.

CHAPTER VI

CRITIQUE OF WHITEHEAD'S THEORY OF KNOWLEDGE

The difficulty always arises in treating of a philosophy as to where to place the theory of knowledge in that philosophy. Our knowledge has a cause which is primarily outside the mind, and from that point of view it might seem better to consider any philosophy's explanation of being before considering how that being is understood. Yet, the mental approach to reality is going to color the entire philosophy of reality, and hence, from this latter point of view, it might seem better to treat of a theory of knowledge before treating a theory of being. In Thomistic philosophy, a theory of being is first considered as being as it exists outside of the mind, and then being as it is known by the mind. There was no professed epistemology in Thomistic philosophy. That arose as a concession to, and a defense against, false theories of knowledge that made philosophy largely epistemology. However, since in the exposition of Whitehead's philosophy we first considered his theory of knowledge, we shall here treat of it first, before passing on to his theory of reality.

As we have seen, Whitehead claims to be a defender of speculative philosophy. He does build up a speculative system. For that, we have only praise and admiration. He works for speculative philosophy in a world of specialized sciences, epistemologies, psychologies, and psychiatries. It is upon his explanation of the knowing process that we shall here differ.

In considering his psychology and epistemology, we have seen that he attempts to keep it in consonance with the entire philosophy of organism. All that he postulates concerning the prehension of actual entities among themselves, by the acceptance or rejection of proferred feelings, he applies to the knowing process. He has hit on a fundamental truth in any epistemology, namely, that there is an attraction of the mind to the known object, based upon a similarity of principles. That, in the long run, is the only explanation of the reason for knowing. The Thomist would say that things are by their very nature knowable and that the mind is by its very nature ordained to know those beings.

Let us now turn to the Thomistic theory of knowledge. This

latter is also based upon experience. It is based upon the objective existence of the external world, the extra-mental world, and the ability of the mind to perceive the objects of this world, draw a mental, immaterial representation of the essential nature of the thing drawn from the illumination of the sense data, through a process known as 'abstraction.'[1] We shall examine these component phases individually and in detail.

Man has always had experience. He is born a creature capable of knowing, but yet not knowing. In him, he has innate tendencies to know, and the development of his knowing unfolds with the development of the physical organisms that aid in the process of knowing, that is, with the brain, the nervous system, and the sense organs. As man lives and acts and is acted upon, he amasses an ever increasing content of facts and factual data. All this we know from experience. We know that as we develop, we know more and more, we amass a greater content of facts about ourselves, our surroundings, and the entire world and the entire activities of the things in the world. This we know either through our own experience or the experience of others which we learn through contact with others or with their recorded experiences. Thus, we do not live in a world of mental isolation. All our knowledge is both individual and social. We learn from our experience and from the experience of others, while others learn from their own experience and the elements of our own experience that we impart to them either by their contact with us or with our recorded experiences. This is obvious, and to deny it is to stultify our reason, deny our experience, admit that history is a lie. It is to end up in utter scepticism and solipsism. It is ultimately to maintain that the individual ego is the only thing in existence, and that every other thing in the world is only an illusion.

But man's experience is not limited merely to facts. Were that true, his knowledge would be more a matter of forgetting than of learning, for we can retain only so much in the conscious mind while the rest sinks into the subconscious. Man also formulates principles.[2] He formulates principles of knowledge. He perceives principles of identity in the appalling army of facts that face him, and he classifies these existent facts according to these principles. The fact that there are certain common features in existent things

[1] *De Verit.* 1, 1; cf. *C. G.*, L. 1, Q. 3.
[2] *S.T.*, P. 1a, Q. 40, A. 3; P. 1a, Q. 85, A. 1.

that justify our classifying them according to their common features is the whole explanation of science. It is paramount to keep in mind that the principles of a science, or any knowlege, is based upon common features of the objects classified, which features either are or are effects of a principle of identity within the known objects, which principle of identity we term 'essence' or 'substance.'

We can illustrate with an example. The biologist examines living things. In following his text books, he accepts and investigates the Aristotelian definition of life as 'self movement.' In these many representatives of living things, he perceives some that remain fixed, manufacture their own food from water and chemicals absorbed in organs which are especially adapted to that purpose by the energy from sunlight. These living things also are fixed in the ground, and grow other organs from a stalk. These he calls plants. Any living thing that manifests the characteristics listed above, he classifies as plants. In other words, from the observation of a limited number of plants, by virtue of their common operations, he formulates a set of rules for recognizing plants. He also does the same for other living creatures, which have similar characteristics in that they too are living, but which differ from plants in that they also have the power of self-locomotion and have rudimentary knowledge. These he calls animals, and from the limited observation of the characteristics of animals, he lays down rules for the immediate recognition and classification of animals.

That is an example of the physical sciences. That, we say, is in the first degree of mental abstraction, in that we get away from every individual case, we abstract from a multitude of individuals, and form general rules of classification according to operations. Thus, we put order and reason into our knowledge. We save a great deal of minute examinations by laying down principles, based upon the principles in the things observed which are the source of the similarity of operations. The fact that the operations in plants are similar, is based upon principles within the plants themselves, which principles are similar and which similar principles give rise to similar operations.

We also know other sciences which treat of more remote principles and which express these principles in symbols. These are the mathematical sciences. Fundamentally, mathematics is based upon number, extension and quantity.³ Man observes that certain definite patterns of numbers, when combined a certain way, will invariably give certain definite patterns of answers. He abstracts from this and gets arithmetic. He also discovers that in certain figures of cubes and areas, he will get certain properties. He abstracts from this and gets geometry. Then, to save a lot of energy, he abstracts from number, and symbolizes it through representative letters. For example, $x + y = z$, can mean $2 + 3 = 5$, or two apples plus three apples are equal to five apples. He can apply these symbols to many, many things and always get the same ratio. He can forget all about the original numbers and calculate entirely in letters. This he calls 'algebra.' When the calculations get into what Whitehead would call 'purely symbolic reference' or in symbolic relations, he discovers a definite pattern of relations, and this science of symbolic relations, when applied to reality—any realities that fall under this pattern of relations—he calls it 'calculus.' When he keeps the relations purely in the abstract state, he calls it 'symbolic logic.' This more remote system of abstraction we term the 'second degree of abstraction.' It is a more remote abstraction from the things themselves. The first degree of abstraction is based upon operations, which are immediately joined to the intrinsic principle of the source of operations in each individual entity. The second degree of abstraction is based upon relations both within entities and between entities, and hence is more remote from the principles within the related entities. Since, thus, mathematics is based upon relations, mathematical philosophers will logically tend towards relativistic philosophies.

Then we meet the 'third degree of abstraction,' wherein we get to the ultimate principles of existing entities. This is philosophy in the full sense. The philosopher does not stop with the operations or the relative patterns of individual things and classed of individual things, although he depends a great deal upon the first and second degrees of abstraction for the data of his ultimate principles. The philosopher asks, especially, three questions: "What?", "How?", "Why?". He asks these questions of each individual being, and of all being in general, so that if he is a great philosopher, he can answer those questions of each and every being that exists.

---

³ *S.T.*. P. 1a, Q. 85, A. 1 ad 2; P. 3a, Q. 77, A. 2 ad 4.

and he can formulate truths that can be applied not only to movable beings, not only to quantified things, but to every thing that is, was, will be, either actually or possibly.[4] He can get down to nature, causes, and purposes of each individual thing, or he can treat of substance, cause, and purpose in the abstract.

And here is the important point that we discover from human experience, namely, that although relatively few men are scientists, relatively few men are mathematicians, every man in sound mind is somewhat of a philosopher, for every man is constantly asking—even from his childhood, and perhaps more so in his childhood—the questions: "What?", "How?" and "Why?" Every man in sound mind can and does answer the questions by saying of whatever thing he is asking, some such remark as, "It acts that way because it is made that way." In other words, every man realizes that his knowledge of things depends upon his knowledge of the intimate nature of the things known. What he does not know is that he is reiterating the basic principle of Thomistic philosophy that being is 'per se' knowable, and the mind is in potency to know the intimate nature of each and every being.

Thus, when St. Thomas, in that magnificent work *De Veritate*, states as a fundamental introduction for the consideration of the nature of truth that everything is in its very nature knowable and that the mind, by its very nature, is essentially ordained to know many things actually and all things potentially,[5] he is merely reiterating two principles that flow directly from experience. If his statement is not true, then everything except the individual ego is a deception, and science and history, all knowledge, all awareness, all experience, all these are an illusion and a fraud. There is no reason for anything. Man's mind, which is constantly seeking reasons, is deceiving itself, and we end in utter, desperate scepticism.

Thus, individual and universal experience show us that we know not only facts, but that our knowledge depends upon our knowledge of the intimate natures of some things. I say the mind knows some things, for history shows us that although we will find a maze of error, still, concerning certain fundamental things all men agree in their knowledge. Through the maze of false theories that have been accepted by men at various times, there filter certain irre-

---
[4] Cf. *C.G.L.* 1, Q. 1.
[5] *De Veritate*, Q. 1, A. 1,

futable truths which in themselves are sufficient to found sciences, philosophies, and systems of ethics.

Briefly, then, experience, which is always the test of our truth although not the norm of it, shows us that in our experience, we know not only facts, but also, principles, insofar as the mind naturally—we might almost say instinctively—seeks constantly a sufficient reason for every item of experience. The questions of childhood and the questions of manhood are sufficient to show that.

Let us now consider the process whereby man acquires those ideas from the wealth of individual things that flood his consciousness. The fact exists that man has a knowledge of facts, a knowledge of what we call 'universal ideas,' and a knowledge of principles. These he acquires through his mental processes. The fact of such knowledge remains, although there are many theories to try to explain the fact.

The Thomistic explanation is to be found in the process of 'abstraction.' Abstraction is the revealing by the mind of the universal element in the individuals that present themselves to the knowing mind. Abstraction presupposes a philosophy of extramental being, the necessity of which we will see in the next chapter. It presupposes that in every individual there is a determinable factor and a determining factor. The determining factor is that which makes a thing what it is in a determined grade of being. Hence, it is common to all members of that species. A special manifestation of the determinable factor, which determinable factor is the principle of limitation, is the principle of numerical individuation in corporeal substances. The determinable factor in general is the principle of limitation. This special manifestation of the determinable factor ('materia quantitate signata') is the principle of individuation. Abstraction, since it treats of universals, reveals the universal factor, specifically, the essence, for since things exist as individual members of species, there must be some principle, some universal principle, of specification, or else the species do not have a reason for their existence as such. There must be something in man whereby he has humanity in common with all other actual and potential men. There must also be some limitation whereby he is *this* man. Abstraction is, in other words, getting away from the principle of individuation in anything.[6] It

---

[6] *De Ente et Essentia*, C. V; cf. *S.T.*, P. 1a, Q. 14, A. 1; *S.T.*, P. 1a, Q. 85, A. 1.

is getting away from the 'thisness' of anything to discover what the thing is in itself. It is getting away from the individual characteristics of *this* man to discover what human nature is in itself.

The learning process is carried on by a twofold set of faculties, the sense faculties and the intellectual faculties. The sense faculties take care of the individuality of the known object, whereas the intellect treats of the universal element in the object.[7] This again flows from the nature of each thing as a union of determining and determinable factors. The determinable factor is matter, and hence the source of the individual characteristics of the thing. The determining factor is the principle—and note, it is a principle,—of universality. The characteristics, or accidents, residing as they do in the matter of the thing, are going to be material. Hence, their counterpart in the learning process is going to be those factors that partake of and treat of the material characteristics, namely, the sense organs. The determining factor, on the other hand, since it is the principle of universalization, transcends matter, and hence will be dealt with by the immaterial element in the learning process, namely, the intellect. Thus, this explanation gives a sufficient reason for the main points under discussion, namely, (i) universal ideas, which transcend the individuals; (ii) the intellect and intellectual knowledge, which are the process whereby we acquire concepts; and (iii) sense organs, insofar as they apprehend the individuality of the thing.

As necessary backgrounds for explanation, we must remember the following factors: (i) matter (the determinable element) is the principle of individuation; (ii) form (the determining element) is the principle of specification; (iii) substance (the union of matter and form in an individual thing) is a *metaphysical* (*not* physical) principle, namely, the principle of identity within the object. It is *not* to be considered as a material, corporeal static entity upholding the characteristics of the thing. Hence, since it is a metaphysical principle, it is knowable by the intellect.

Just what is the process whereby the sense apprehension of a multitude of individual entities becomes intellectual knowledge of the essence of things? As mentioned above, it is abstraction, and contains the following components.

1. *Sense Knowledge.* Individual objects as we know them con-

---

[7] *S.T.*, P. 1a, Q. 12, A. 13; 1a, Q. 85, A. 1.

tain many characteristics which are either material, or which are closely allied to the material. All of them, except operation (which also has a relation to the individuality of the thing, and hence to matter), can be reduced to quantity, quality, and relation. These characteristics give off qualities (such as color, sound,—which are in themselves physical) which are apprehended by sense objects which have as their proper objects the qualities given off the thing.[8] For example, size is known by color, for by color, the thing is apprehended by the eye and its magnitude is thus apparent. Proximity can be measured either by light (color) or by sound. The sense objects which apprehend the qualities of the individual thing are the eye (for color), the ear (for sound), the nose (for odor), the tongue (for taste), and the organs of touch.

Each of the senses receives its stimulus, and transmits it to the brain. Thus, in many individual objects, there are several separate images, according to the several sense organs by which the object is apprehended. For example, a symphony orchestra can be apprehended by the eye and by the ear, other objects by more senses. These several images of the same object are then fused into one composite image of the object, and to explain this, the 'common sense'[9] is postulated. (Note, that this is not the popular notion of 'common sense' which is a manifestation of prudence.) This composite image, or 'phantasm' as it is called, still remains an image. It is still a particular representation of a particular object. It may be enriched by the sentient imagination, or by the sensient memory; it may also be combined with other images of the same type of object, but even this composite image still remains particular, because it is still limited by the individualities of the objects of the fused image. Furthermore, and primarily, *it is not an explanation. It does not give a sufficient reason. It still remains an image. The universal is universal because it understands the object. It reaches to the sufficient reason of the object.* Hence, sense knowledge, important as it is for data, is not the ultimate in the explanation of things. We must, then, postulate another faculty to explain our understanding of things, and this faculty is the intellect.

2. *Intellectual Knowledge.* We know from experience that we

---

[8] *S.T.*, P. 1a, Q. 78, A. 3; cf. *II Sent. D. 2*, Q. 2 ad 5; *Qq. Dd. De Anima*, A. 15; *De Anima*, L. III, lect. 7.

[9] Cf. *S.T.*, P. 1a, Q. 78, A. 4; cf. *Qq. Dd. De Anima*, A. 13.

have ideas, and that our ideas transcend the limitations of space and time. Our idea of human nature is not limited to any man, nor to any composite image of men. Our idea of man is an understanding of man's nature, which certainly is not an image of many men. How, then, do we get this understanding of man's nature, or of the nature of anything? We have seen that sense knowledge is insufficient. We realize that we must have some mental faculty to gain that understanding, and this faculty we call the 'intellect.' In treating of the intellect, we have two problems facing us: (i) how do we gain our concepts? and (ii) where are our concepts retained? For this, we must postulate the 'intellectus agens'[10] (active intellect) and the 'intellectus possibilis' (possible intellect). Let us examine the function of each.

The active intellect bridges the gap between the individual object, in all its singularity, and the universal idea. This must not be understood as making something spiritual out of something material. Nowhere in the process does the material become the spiritual. It is not a process of the diminution of materiality and the corresponding increase of spirituality. It is, instead, a process where the knowing mind illuminates by concentrating the attention on a knowable, metaphysical principle within the phantasm of the known object. It is the process whereby the intellect recognizes the accidental to be accidental and to be the effect of a deeper principle which *is* the thing, a principle of identity within the thing that makes the thing what it is. It is a process of by-passing characteristics to the understanding of the very nature of the thing.[11]

Hence in this process of intellectual comprehension on the part of the active intellect, the intellect seizes upon the phantasm, and by a process of concentration, produces the intelligible species, a means whereby the mind knows the nature of the individual by reflection. It would be, for example, seizing upon the phantasm of an individual man, recognizing his size, qualities, etc., to be merely accidents, and getting down to the understanding of the human nature within him.

The work of the active intellect is the process of a knowing mind revealing or illuminating a knowable metaphysical principle. Hence, there is a perfect parallelism between the nature of a thing as knowable

---

[10] *S.T.*, p. 1a, Q. 79, A. 3 and 4; cf. *Qq. Dd. De Anima*, A. 4.
[11] Cfr. *S.T.* 1, 12, 13; 1, 85, 1.

and the nature of a thing as known. The concept that results from the action of the active intellect is known as the 'species impressa.' The 'species impressa' is properly in the 'possible intellect' wherein it is retained. However, the possible intellect is more than a storehouse for concepts. Whereas the active intellect was the means of illustrating the sense image, the possible intellect is the scene of most of our intellectual activity, especially of judging and reasoning. The concept as it comes from the active intellect enters into the possible intellect where it is enriched with associated knowledge drawn from the intellectual memory, for example, principles which will apply to this concept, etc. This is called the 'species expressa' because it is not only a representation of the object to which it corresponds, but is also the full and expressive understanding of every member of the class of being to which the object belongs. Thus, our universal idea of man can be applied to every man actual or potential. Our idea of beauty can be applied to any and every beautiful object. This is so because our idea is now an understanding of the nature of the thing, a comprehension of an intelligible principle, a metaphysical principle that is the 'whatness' of every member of the class of being that the idea represents.

It is a faithful idea, because it is an understanding.[12] Since it is a faithful idea, as the member of a judgment, the judgment can be true, since it is founded on the natures of objective things and is not merely mental gymnastics. Thus it is that we can say: "All men are mortal. Socrates is a man. Therefore, Socrates is mortal." We can understand all men without counting every individual man (as John Stuart Mill would have us do) because we do not stop with the varying accidentals or operations, but we get down to the universal principle within every man. In the light of that, we can understand that Socrates is a man, because we recognize that he shares that universal principle of manhood, and hence we can predicate of him what we predicate of all men.

What shall we say of this process of abstraction? If we accept now what we shall see later that being exists, then abstraction is the soundest and most adequate explanation of our knowing. It is the ultimate answer to all knowledge. Knowledge, as we have seen above, has no meaning if we do not accept as a basic principle

---

[12] *S.T.*, P. 1a, Q. 84, A. 1; cf. P. 1a, Q. 85, A. 1 and 1. Cf. *De Verit.*, Q. 1, A. 1; *S.T.*, P. 1a, Q. 88, A. s.

that beings are by their nature knowable, and the mind is by its very nature ordained to know. It gives the sufficient reason for our awareness of (i) the stability of things; (ii) our universal ideas; (iii) our universal principles (upon which *all* science is built); (iv) the faithful correspondence between our ideas and the things as they exist; and (v) as a sequence of (iv), the unity of human knowledge upon the fundamentals of thinking and living.

The last two points are important. If our knowledge is not a faithful representation of reality, if it is solely the product of the mind without dependence upon the natures of things as they exist outside of the mind, then knowledge is going to change with the vagaries of the individual knowing minds. Yet, we know that such is not the case, for in that case, all social intercourse would be out of the question. To object that the minds can be the same while the external world changes does not answer the problem, for we can further inquire, where do we get knowledge of the natures of minds other than our own? From the outside. To deny that is to affirm solipsism.

Now, if the mind is our tool for understanding the natures of things, our theory of knowledge is going to shape our understanding and explanation of extra-mental entities. Briefly, it amounts to this. We have unified knowledge. That unified knowledge means nothing unless the mind can faithfully represent objectivity. Since the mind faithfully represents objectivity, the operations of the mind can be taken as a guide as to the nature of things. Which means, that *if the mind so operates that it supposes a philosophy of being and yet understands and proclaims a philosophy of becoming, the philosophy is inconsistent.* And that, I think, will be the basis of our critique of Whitehead's theory of knowledge.

We have seen that Whitehead's theory of knowledge is empirical. It is based upon facts, which Whitehead terms 'actual entities' or 'actual occasions,' and which he defines as 'items of experience.' We can say, at the outset, that we agree with much of what Whitehead maintains in his philosophy of knowledge. We shall disagree with him as we would disagree with all empiricists, namely, in maintaining that he does not go far enough. Furthermore, like all empiricists, he exceeds his empiricism. By the very fact that he attempts to give a speculative explanation, he exceeds the limits of empiricism, and thus, is inconsistent. By that fact, his empiricism is insufficient and inconsistent.

Points of Agreement With Whitehead's Theory of Knowledge

Although we disagree with Whitehead's peculiar use of traditional terms, we shall let that pass. We shall agree with him in his explanation of 'presentational immediacy,' 'symbolic reference' and 'causal efficacy.' Much of what he says about 'feelings' in analogous to our notion of natural appetites and natural functions.

Whitehead's doctrine on 'symbolic reference' is quite similar to our theory of sense knowledge. What he calls 'presentational immediacy' we call sense awareness. What he terms 'casual efficacy' we call the operation of the internal senses.

Speaking of 'presentational immediacy' Whitehead states that it is the immediate perception of the contemporary external world appearing as an element in our own experience. We see the world as a community of factors just as actual as we ourselves. Here, Dr. Whitehead is to be highly commended for his realism. He is a champion of realism as opposed to the clumsy attempts to explain reality on the part of idealists, especially on the part of the disciples of German idealism, the Fichtian and Hegelian causing of the non-ego by the ego. Dr. Whitehead starts, as is natural to man's thinking, from the ground up, from the external to the internal. He does not cripple philosophy by the question, "Can we know?" He refreshingly asserts, "We can know, directly."

Furthermore, with us, he agrees that we have specialized organs, the senses, for the purpose of perceiving stimuli from the things known. These things exist actually, and emit (so to speak) stimuli to which our senses react. He would have it that the 'feelings' of the thing perceived and the 'feelings' of the perceiving sense formulate the data for us. That is quite similar to our notion that the sense is at first stimulated by the data from the perceived object, and then reacts to the stimuli. Whitehead's notion of 'feelings' in lower entities, analogous to perception in the higher entities, is similar to our notions of tropisms in lower living things, and natural appetites in inorganic beings.

In the objects perceived, we again agree with Whitehead. He says that we see a community of things as actual as ourselves. We too maintain that we perceive a number of actualities that are not ourselves. We see them extended in space by reason of their own extended character.

Lastly, on this point, we agree with Whitehead that sense perception alone—or, as Whitehead would term it, 'bare presentational immediacy'—shows process more than being. Bare sense perception shows us what he would call 'functional activity.' A stimulus is here, is gone, but leaves an impression. Our senses are being stormed by such stimuli, to which they are constantly reacting in pattern after pattern. For example, the eye now perceives this, that, the other thing, all in the duration of a few seconds. Thus, it is all functional activity, even in bare sense knowledge.

The permanent element—or quasi permanent element—comes in the union of all sense data by the associative sense, and the enrichment of all by the other internal senses (sense memory and sense imagination). The understanding comes from the intellect. This function of the internal senses is what Whitehead terms 'symbolic reference' which has as its twofold function (i) enrichment of sense data with past sense data (sense memory) and (ii) localization of the cause of the data. This is brought about, as we saw, by 'causal efficacy.'

From mere 'presentational immediacy' we do not know much. We know facts, but we observe neither sequence nor principle to them. We cannot see the principles in things merely by observation. We must bring past experience to explain and to give depth to present awareness. It is 'causal efficacy' (or as we should say, 'memory') that does this. By past experience, it identifies the things outside us, by showing that one is a quality, the other a cause, by applying sweetness to the rose and sound to the bell. Again, it thereby indicates the cause of the awareness, and thereby shows us the order and causality in nature. ("For we can only understand causation in terms of our observations of these occasions.")[13]

POINTS OF DISAGREEMENT

We may now note a certain inconsistency in Whitehead's explanation of knowledge proper. 'Causal efficacy' should mean the recognition of the cause of knowledge. 'Symbolic reference' should mean the referring of symbols to things known as a means of recognition and understanding. Yet, 'causal efficacy' seems to be limited to the recognition of things as part of past experience. It is a means of recognition rather than of understanding. It is

---

[13] *Adventures of Ideas*, p. 237.

all a part of direct experience. Intellectual knowledge, with Whitehead, is limited to speculation.

In the Thomistic explanation, recognition of a thing is sensitive, achieved by awareness and sense memory. Understanding of the thing, as well as speculation, is intellectual. Whitehead has to admit either that 'causal efficacy' is an intellectual faculty much as our active intellect, or he must admit that there is no true abstract idea, only a fused image, because from a sense faculty alone a concept cannot result. Yet, experience shows that we have knowledge of abstract ideas, and Whitehead claims to be a champion of speculative knowledge. He attributes to 'causal efficacy' many of the functions of the active intellect, and yet explains it *not* by an understanding of the thing, but by enrichment of sense data by memory. It is true that memory *helps* understanding, but intellectual memory also *presupposes* understanding and depends upon understanding. If 'causal efficacy' is the principle of understanding as Whitehead seems to say, he has the order reversed, for he is saying that memory is the cause of present understanding. The past is the cause of the future. Note the consistency with Whitehead's notion of objective causality. This is ultimately empiricism. Whitehead's notion of understanding through perception is inadequate in its failure to distinguish clearly the essential difference between sense and intellectual consciousness. According to the Scholastic viewpoint, the latter far more completely explains the universal fact that we *understand* things, as well as have consciousness of them.

The inadequacy of Whitehead's theory of intellection is further seen when we turn to his notion of the intellect. He himself considers the work of the intellect to be symbolism. That represents his mathematical viewpoint. Knowledge for him is functional. It consists in formulating relations, mathematical symbols, which are then applied to theories of reality. Hence, knowledge is outgoing. That may explain his love for 'feeling' in knowledge, and his application of it to reality. It is obvious from human experience that feelings are out-going. Furthermore, the invasion of emotions into the field of knowledge, which frequently occurs, usually results in subjectivism if consistently followed.

Whitehead's theory of intellection is limited to judgment, and we remember that he agrees with Locke's notion of judgments being made *before* the thing is known. It is, if we may put it this way, a feeling of yes, no, or maybe. 'Intuitive judgments' are the 'yes' or 'no' judgments, while 'suspended judgments' are the 'maybe' judgments. As we have seen, Whitehead's explanation of these judgments is highly complicated. To explain the obvious fact of experience that we know things, and naturally, as part of the thousands of things that make up a day's experience, and also to avoid the a priorism of Hume and Kant, he marshals an imposing array of feelings that imply a mutual interchange of mental natural appetites with the natural appetites of non-mental realities. 'Intuitional judgments' allow us, by way of feelings, to judge concerning facts. Since the other type of judgments is 'suspended judgments,' we are led to the conclusion that we cannot judge concerning principles. If that is the case, then Whitehead's theory of knowledge is at variance with human experience and with itself.

It is inconsistent with itself. We have seen the empiricism in Whitehead's epistemology. If a man follows this theory of knowledge, he must logically be led to the conclusion that he cannot formulate principles. Yet, Whitehead's whole philosophy is a formulation of principles. If a man is an empiricist, he must distrust speculative reasoning. Yet, Whitehead's aim, in trying to philosophize about 'every item of experience' is to overcome the prevalent distrust of speculative reasoning. He is, of set purpose, determined to restore philosophy to its proper place in a world of scientific specialization. Yet he uses the methods of science, and limits himself to the first (physical) and second (mathematical) degrees of abstraction.

We have seen that 'symbolic reference,' the process whereby we know, is empirical. That fails to answer the problem of where we get our universal immaterial ideas of the natures of things. Whitehead would say from the interplay of sense awareness and memory. Yes, but sense awareness only gives us images, and if memory is to clarify experience with ideas, the ideas must come from somewhere. That means that there must be a process that abstracts the metaphysical principle from the sense image. Sense awareness itself does not present an idea. Whitehead agrees with us on that. Memory, then, cannot get an idea that transcends the image from 'causal efficacy' unless that idea be innate, as the a priorists would hold. Yet Whitehead rejects the a priorists, and will only grant to them what we are willing to grant to them, that the subjective element (which has already depended upon the outside for all knowledge) clarifies the sense data now presented. Here is the difference: *Thomism has a sufficient reason whereby we can explain the attaining of the idea from the image,* namely, that in the thing is a principle, a metaphysical principle, of identity, which is in its very nature knowable, and that the mind has power to know and understand that principle and use it in judgments. To deny that is to commit intellectual suicide, for it is to deny the knowing process, which denial ends up in an entirely repugnant solipsism. Whitehead has no such sufficient reason.

Whitehead's theory of the attainment of knowledge ('symbolic reference') is inconsistent with experience. We do have universal ideas. We do know things. We do judge of things. That is not only the basis of all our knowledge, but also of all our science, even of all our life. The conducting of our whole life is based upon the fact that we *know, understand, judge,* and *apply* not only facts, but also principles. To deny that, because of empiricism, is again to deny everything. Hence, the Scholastic theory of knowledge is not merely a speculative explanation of the experience of knowing, but also a vital principle in the explanation of all life.

Whitehead's theory of judgment is again inconsistent with itself and inconsistent with experience. It is inconsistent with experience, because we not only judge of things and ideas, but we also judge among ideas. This, too, is part of every phase of life, not merely of knowledge and science.

It is inconsistent with itself, because it is not rational. It is sublimated empiricism, and for that matter, identical with experience, for it is based upon the same principle of the empirical acquisition of knowledge, peculiar to Whitehead's philosophy of feelings. Hence the judging process cannot transcend, as Whitehead would have it do, the process of learning. They are both based upon feelings. If it be objected that the operation of the intellect transcends the acquisition of knowledge because the feelings themselves transcend the feeling of experience, the gap is still unexplained between images and ideas about which we judge. Whitehead still fails to explain the origin of ideas, which origin is simply and metaphysically explained by the Thomistic doctrine of the active intellect.

Hence, we shall see, that ultimately, to explain the experience we have that we *know things, judge things,* and *judge principles,* we shall have to depend upon a philosophy of *being.*

Thus it is that the theory of knowledge is the measure of a philosophy. It is the tool whereby a man measures the world. If the tool is defective, a man's explanation of reality will be concomitantly defective. Of course, unless a man follows an a prioristic philosophy, his epistemology will be the effect of his experience. But also, if this epistemology is superficial, his philosophy of reality is bound to be similar.

Is this the case with Whitehead's philosophy? I think so. His philosophy of knowing is limited to the first and second degrees of abstraction. The senses perceive primarily accidents and operations, appearances and change. Whitehead's philosophy is one of becoming. His theory of judgment is in the second degree of abstraction, mathematical. He sums it up in symbolism, that is, applying symbols to reality and to ideas. Mathematical symbols are patterns of relation. Whitehead's philosophy is relativistic. Hence, he ends in dynamic monism wherein all is process that is ordered by mathematical forms. It is Platonism brought up to date. Whitehead differs from other relativists in that he projects vitalism into reality. This is a modern version of Leibniz's organic unity through the instrumentality of Whiteheadian 'feelings.' From empiricism, he makes the ultimate reality the 'actual entity,' or 'actual occasion' which is an 'item of experience.' From his mathematical symbolism he makes the ultimate principle 'creativity.' This latter is a relativistic orderly process with mathematical symbols as the principle of order.

He leaves unanswered the sufficient reason for the knowability of things, the sufficient reason for our knowing of things. Both are problems of reality, of life, of human experience. The Thomistic theory of knowledge offers an answer to those problems by giving a sufficient reason for them. It bases itself upon extramental being which is by its nature knowable and a mind which is by its nature capable of knowing the intrinsic principles of things.

Nevertheless Whitehead deserves a certain credit. Some phases of his philosophy are evidently superficial but Whitehead himself is not a superficial thinker. He has had the courage and vision to break the limitations of science and to attempt a speculative explanation of reality, free from the limitations of a priorism. He based himself upon every day experience. This is definitely to his credit. The fault lies not with Whitehead, but with his philosophical heritage.

CHAPTER VII

A Critique of Whitehead's Philosophy of Being and Becoming

As we have seen, a philosophy, in order to be called a philosophy, must attempt to explain the ultimate principles of reality. If it does not do so, it is only a system of general knowledge or a specialized science. A philosophy must investigate the fundamental and ultimate principles of all reality, and then interpret all reality in the light of those principles. Hence, a philosophy must be abstract, and yet a source of interpretation. Needless to say, a philosophy must be true. Its principles must agree with reality. Furthermore, although abstract, it must be in touch with reality. Although necessarily speculative, it must also be practical, for practice is not opposed to speculation, but the fruit of speculation. Thus it is that the Greeks formulated the axiom: "Philosophy is the Guide of Life."

Whitehead is to be admired in that in a world of specialization he attempts to formulate a philosophy truly as such. He tends to break away from the bonds of specialized sciences, and tries to formulate principles wherein we may correctly interpret every item of experience. Furthermore, he attempts to explain all reality through this philosophy. How correct he is in doing so we shall see in this chapter, wherein we shall investigate his explanation of the ultimate principles of reality.

We may state that the ultimate principles in any philosophy are stability and change, or as the Thomistic philosopher would term them, being and becoming. These are the explanation of the fundamental problem of the One and the Many, that is to say, in what way all reality is one, and in what way it is many.

Let us look at the Thomistic philosophy of being and becoming. The great scholastics, Albert, St. Thomas Aquinas, and John Duns Scotus, were Aristotelians. Alexander of Hales and St. Bonaventure were affected by Aristotelianism, although since there were warm admirers of St. Augustine, they were rather Neo-Platonists. Of all the Scholastics, St. Thomas is undoubtedly the greatest. He was fortunate in that he was familiar with Aristotle both through the philosophies and commentaries of such great

Aristotelians as Al Farabi, Avicenna, Averroes, Al Gazal, and Moses Maimonides. Further, he was great enough to see what truth existed in the philosophies of these men and to take advantage of it. He was also fortunate enough and scientific enough to make use of recently discovered Greek texts of Aristotle, and to make best use of the work done upon these by William of Moerbeke. Hence, St. Thomas was peculiarly equipped to be the greatest protagonist of the metaphysics of Aristotle.

St. Thomas could have turned to no greater master than Aristotle for the correct explanation of being and becoming. Aristotle had steered the middle course between the philosophy of Parmenides, which had emphasized being and proclaimed becoming an illusion, and that of Heraclitus, which emphasized becoming and proclaimed being an illusion. In accomplishing this, Aristotle maintained a middle course, so to speak. Whereas Plato was an idealist, starting from ideals and working down to reality, Aristotle, scientist that he was (undoubtedly the greatest scientist of his day), started with knowable reality and worked up to metaphysical principles. St. Thomas used Aristotelianism to put reason to work for faith, and hence formulated as no one did before him or after him a philosophy of revelation.

The question arises, is Thomism true, especially in its explanation of reality? Just what is its explanation? For answer, we must turn to the works of St. Thomas. Particularly valuable, for the totality of Thomism, are the *Summa Theologica*, the *Summa Contra Gentiles*. For particular questions, his shorter works (opuscula) such as *De Ente et Essentia*, *De Principiis Naturae*, and such *Quaestiones Disputatae* as *De Potentia* and *De Veritate*, are of prime importance.

The Thomistic explanation of reality begins with experience. St. Thomas insists that our knowledge begins with the senses,[1] and from the senses we arrive, by reasoning, at our understanding and explanation of reality. As we have already noted, man perceives change by his senses, noting also a certain amount of stability. This is a summary of the beginnings of Greek philosophy and posits man perceiving order in change rather than man perceiving change in order.

Man perceives two things in this change: (i) that things change,

---

[1] *Summa Contra Gentiles*, L. 1, c. 3.

and (ii) that there must be an explanation or sufficient reason for this change. Concerning the former, we may say that the ordinary man rarely comes to the conclusion that all is change. That conclusion is left for certain philosophers. Man almost instinctively knows that there are beings which change. As to the second, man is never satisfied to stop with perceiving orderliness in change. He desires an explanation of that change. Whereas he *perceives* change, he wishes to *know* the reason or reasons behind it. He has a natural, sometimes driving, desire to know the explanations of things.

In searching out the explanation of things, the reason behind the orderliness in change, man identifies things. He works from operations which are specifically different to principles of operation which are thus specifically different. By his senses, he perceives operations and properties. He notices that in different entities these operations and properties differ. By his intellect, his natural faculty of knowing, he passes from these specifically different operations and properties to their principle. He passes from phenomena to noumena. His reasoning is 'a posteriori,' that is to say, from principiates to principles, from effects to causes. Thus it is that men arrive at the notion and existence of 'substance' as the sufficient reason and sufficient explanation of operations and properties.

It is important to remember that substance is a principle. It has been constantly misunderstood, due to the influence of Occam, Descartes, Locke, Hume, and Kant, to be an inert something underlying the accidents. That is not the Thomistic notion of substance. The Thomistic definition of substance is 'that whose nature is to exist in its own right and not in another' (id cui competit existere in se and non in alio). Substance must be active, or it cannot be the principle of action. The Thomists have a principle, 'the operation of a thing is according to the being of the thing' (operatio sequitur esse). Now, if a thing operates it is active. Activity is apparent to the senses. It is everywhere obvious. Modern physics proves that everything is active, and to a certain extent, radioactive. Hence, the principle of things (the 'esse') must be active. Activity does not come from an inert principle. Such would not even be knowable. Hence, when Whitehead inveighs against substance as an inert principle, he is not arguing against the Thomistic notion of substance but against a Lockian or Cartesian notion. For the Thomist, substance must be active, or else there is no sufficient reason for undeniable change.

Thus, according to Thomistic philosophy, composite substance (which we must always remember is *not* inert, but rather a principle of identity within the changing thing) is the key to the explanation of change. How is this explained, and how can we say that there are beings which change rather than simply that there is change? This we find in the Scholastic notion of substance composed of 'act' and 'potency.'

For an explanation of act and potency we must draw upon St. Thomas rather than upon Aristotle. Aristotle explained local motion and the changes in bodies by act and potency. He was correct, of course, but he did not go far enough. St. Thomas took the metaphysical notions of act and potency and applied them to all things, except God, in such a way that he proves from reason what is given to us in revelation that there is an infinite gap between God and contingent beings.

Act is defined as 'a perfection actually existing.' We may note that this expression is not properly a definition. Act, existing things, are so obvious that words are inadequate to define them. Potency is twofold, active and passive. We must note that potency must be considered as a *real* capacity. Active potency, then, may be defined as 'a real capacity to confer a perfection' or 'a principle of action.' Passive potency is defined as 'a real capacity to receive a perfection.' How true are these definitions?[2] Again, we must rationalize from experience.

We see things constantly changing,—ourselves, for instance. Yet, we know that in that change, there is a stable element. We know that we change every moment of the day. We know that we grow old, and as we do so, we are acquiring and losing perfections. Yet, we ourselves remain as the subject of that change. We know that the change is both active and passive. We do things, and things are done to us. The same may be said of every element of our experience, everything we know. If things change, if they act and receive the effects of action, they must have the capacity to do so. If there is constant gain and constant loss, the thing that gains and loses must have the capacity to gain and lose. This capacity we call potency. We know, for example, that we

---

[2] *C.G.* L.I, C. 16; cf. *S.T.* P. 1a, Q. 2, A. 3; P. 1a, Q. 4, A. 2 and 3.

Critique of Whitehead's Theory of Being and Becoming

have the capacity to act in a certain way, although as a matter of fact we do not do so. We also know that we have the capacity to receive a perfection, although we are not so receiving. Yet the active and passive capacities really exist in us.

Potency stands partway between nothing and something. We see from history of philosophy that to deny potency is to fall into one of two schools, static monism, which states that there is only act, and that change (or becoming) is an illusion; and dynamic monism, which states that there is only change, and that being is an illusion.

What are the dangers that arise from falling into monism? Is monism merely an over-simplification or are there truly philosophical (and consequent theological and ethical) dangers in it? We must answer that monism is not only *not* a sufficient explanation of reality, but that it is a dangerous philosophy, both because of its incompleteness and because of its dangerous consequences throughout every field of philosophy and every phase of life. This is no idle statement. It demands investigation.

Monism may be of two kinds: static monism, which claims that all is being; that there is no becoming; that becoming is merely an illusion. The second is dynamic monism, which states that all is change; that there is no being; that being is merely an illusion.

What are the dangers inherent in these philosophies? We may say, briefly, that static monism makes everything absolute, whereas dynamic monism makes everything relative. Neither allows for division into entities. Both deny that the individual entities that exist are anything else than the ultimate principle. Both, to be consistent, must maintain that each and every entity *is* the ultimate principle. Hence, then, both deny that anything may be caused. Rather, *if both are consistent with their principles*, both deny that anything can be caused. Of course, both will try to include causality within their philosophy, but their explanations of causality will be inconsistent with the principles of their philosophy.

Let us first investigate static monism to see how it denies division and causality. There are two ways in which a thing may be said to be. We may say that the nature of the thing is simply to be. We make its nature identical with existence. If that is so, it has within itself no principle of diversity from any and every other thing that exists. If the nature of each and every thing is existence, since all things exist, then all things are the same, all things are one, of identical nature, namely, existence. Hence, there are not many but only one. There is no division for there is no reason for division.

Furthermore, if existence is the nature of each and every thing, there is no reason of non-being in them.[3] They cannot not-be. They are not indifferent as to being or non-being. There is no non-being. Hence, there is no change, for change implies a transition from non-being to being. Since there is no change, there can be no cause, for a cause is a principle whereby something passes from non-being into being. According to this theory, change or becoming is an illusion. Why? Because a thing, in order to change, must come into being. That is to say, a thing must be and not-be.

Thus, in static monism, there is no differentiation between entities, nor is there any becoming, and hence, no causality. But, if there is no differentiation, if all things *are* without any distinction in their natures, if, then, all things are the same, there is no difference between God and creatures. This follows from a twofold development. First, there is no difference between God and creatures because there is no difference in their natures. By their natures they are the same, for the nature of both God and creature is simply to be. Secondly, creatures cannot not-be. Hence, like God, they are absolutely necessary. Thus, Spinoza, a follower of static monism, is thoroughly logical in saying that all things are God and God is all things, univocally. Pantheism is the logical result of static monism.

The second way in which a thing may be said to be is to say that it *has* existence, that it participates in existence according to its nature. Each thing in existence does not exhaust being. It shares it. This implies limitation. If a thing does not exhaust being, it is limited. Since it is limited by its nature, it is divided off from every other being. This implies two things: (i) the capacity of a thing to exist (potency), and (ii) its existence (act). Hence, in order to explain differentiation and division of being, a composition of potency and act is required.[4]

Furthermore, the participation of something in existence implies cause. If a thing *participates* in being, if it *shares* being,—if, in

---

[3] Cf. *Summa Theologica*, P. 1a, Q. 54, A. 1; cf. *C.G.*, L. II, c 52; *I Sent. D.* 3, Q. 1, A. 1 ff.

[4] *S.T.* I, 9, 1; cf. *I Sent.* D. 8, Q. 3, A. 1; *De Ente et Essentia* C. V.

short, it exists *analogically* and not univocally,—then it has the reason of its being not in itself, but in something else. It is contingent. Hence, it must be caused. This likewise implies potency and act.[5]

What of dynamic monism? This postulates that all is becoming and that being is an illusion. If the essence of everything is to become, then everything is the same. Any differentiation between entities is only a point of view. Each entity has the same reason of its essence, namely, to become. Hence, within each thing there is no principle of differentiation. Any differentiation in a flowing stream of becoming is that of a mental point of view. Hence, the only differences are events of becoming, occasions of flux.

In a consistent philosophy of becoming there can be no causation. Cause means that something comes into *being*. But if there is no being, there is no sufficient reason for a cause, no need for a cause. Thus, again, a being must be composite to be caused. If each thing is becoming and if becoming is the ultimate principle, then becoming is the sufficient reason for the existence of the entity, and there is no need to go outside of the thing for its sufficient reason. It is in view of that that we must interpret what Whitehead has to say and what he means by 'self-causation.'

However, a philosophy of becoming, a dynamic monism, is inconsistent with itself. It tries to explain stability, differentiation, and causation. These facts are patent in experience. It must explain them either in terms of becoming or in terms of being. If it elects to do the former, it should really have no need to do so, for if becoming is the sufficient reason of all things, there can be no differentiation, stability, causation. If it elects to do the latter, it must explain these in terms of either nothing or being. It cannot do so in the former, hence it must turn to being wherein it is no longer a dynamic monism. To reduce the ultimate reason of everything to becoming without being, or to say that what we call being is really becoming, is to eventuate in a contradiction.[6]

Dynamic monism is dangerous because it gives no real basis for values. It eliminates the foundation of religion, God, by making Him either the ultimate becoming or a subordinate phase in the ultimate process. All other values, likewise, are but phases of

---

[5] *De Ente et Essentia*, C. V; cf. *S.T.* 1, 3, 4; 1, 3, 7; I, 44, 1; *C.G.* II, 15.

[6] Aristotle, *Met.* XI, 6; 1063a18; cfr. *In. XI Met. Lect.* II, 2234, 2243; *De Pot.* Q. 3, A. 3; *S.T.* Ia, 45, 3.

becoming, and hence have no permanent value. There can be no ethics when there are shifting standards, vagaries of the force of circumstances. Certainly the history of ethics has borne that out, in morality, in law, in economics. Even the expression 'shifting values' is a contradiction in terms. Hence any philosophy of becoming is inconsistent with itself when it sets up permanent standards of ethics.

Dynamic monism, just like static monism, is to be refuted from the doctrine of potency and act, determinability and determining. This was done incipiently by Plato, definitely by Aristotle, and completely by St. Thomas. Let us now turn to the doctrine of potency and act as advanced by St. Thomas to see how it guarantees and explains being and becoming.

Plato tried to discover a middle ground between static monism and dynamic monism by postulating 'being which exists and is determined,' and 'being, which in a certain way exists but is not determined.'[7] Aristotle clarified the issue by postulating potency, or really existing capacities.

How does potency explain change? In two ways: (a) it shows how we cannot have created being without change, and (b) it shows how we cannot have change without being. The former also explains the limitations of being, and shows how beings are contingent, that is to say, why they have within them the principles whereby they change. Let us take the former first.

We know of no being (except God) that does not change, and that is not limited in some way or other. We know of no absolutely necessary being (again, except God). Every being that we know comes into being, exists for a time, and passes away.[8] Even the poet's 'eternal hills' are constantly changing, constantly deteriorating. We know that there was a time when they were not, and we know that they will cease to exist, and that at present they are constantly changing in some way. The scientist tells us how the universe came into being, what its present course is, and assures us that it will pass away. And why? Because every being is limited by its capacities. A thing cannot exceed its capacities or potencies.

Each thing exists according to its nature, its concrete individual nature. John Smith exists as John Smith and differently than William Jones. A man exists differently than a dog. Plants exist

---
[7] Plato, the *Sophist*, 241d, 257a, 259c.
[8] *S.T.*, P. 1a, Q. 9, A. 1; cf. P. 1a, Q. 2, A. 3.

differently than inorganic things. In other words, each thing, in reference to existence, cannot exceed its capacity for existence. Thus, its capacity divides it off from the rest of existing beings. If such were not the case, if it were its own existence, unlimited, it would be all of existence. But that is obviously absurd. Things are what they are and do not exhaust existence. They share it.[9]

Furthermore, each thing is not only limited in reference to existence, but also in reference to the perfections it receives. A dog cannot receive the perfections beyond dog nature. Despite the assertions of animal lovers, we have never yet known a horse to enjoy a joke. Why? Because it is beyond horse nature to have an intellectual appreciation of the incongruous. A man is not a pure spirit. Why? Because it is beyond his nature to be so. A man can have neither the swiftness or agility of the swallow nor can he attain the size of a whale. Why? Because it is beyond his capacities to attain the qualities of the former and the quantity of the latter.

Hence, a thing's essence is its capacity to partake in existence, and in reference to existence, its nature is a potency that cannot be exceeded. A thing cannot receive more existence than its capacities allow. Similarly, a thing's capacities forbid its receiving more accidental perfections than are according to those capacities or potencies. In other words, potency, passive potency, is the principle of limitation, and shows how there are gradations in beings, shows how each thing is neither all of being nor all of existence.

To summarize the above:[10] if a thing is limited, as all things obviously are, it is contingent. If it is contingent, it had a beginning and will usually have an end. Only the absolutely necessary has neither beginning nor end. We can formulate it logically thus: a thing either changes or does not change. But in order not to change, it must be unlimited, absolutely necessary. Such is not the case, since in being what it is it is limited. Hence, it changes. In other words, the obvious fact of change is explained in the limitation of things by passive potency.

Potency and Act guarantee Being. We must note that change presupposes something that changes. The whole proof for change as outlined above, is based upon existing natures. This is the second requirement of change, namely, that we must have changing

---

[9] *De Ente et Essentia*, C. V.
[10] *S.T.*, P. 1a, Q. 2, A. 3.

things. Change is not a sufficient explanation of itself. This is again a matter of potencies.

Let us see what occurs in change. First of all, what do we mean by change? We may define change as 'the transition of a thing from one state of being to a different state of being.' That implies three terms. There is the prior state, the state achieved, and the subject which passes from one to the others.[11] Can we have change which exists subsistently in its own right or must we have a subject of change? The scholastic philosophers maintain that we must have a subject of change, that change cannot subsist in its own right. Certainly from human experience we cannot conceive of change without something that changes. But is there a metaphysical proof for this?

Again, we must consider the components of change. We have the 'terminus a quo' (which we may call the point of departure), the 'terminus ad quem' (which we may call the point of arrival), and something in between. The actual process of change implies the loss of the point of departure and the gain of the point of arrival. Hence, change consists of loss, gain, and the subject which loses and gains. Now, if we eliminate the subject, we are faced with the following dilemma: in change, we either have loss and gain identified, or else we have loss and gain separate. If we have them identified, we have that which is loss and not-loss, or gain and not-gain simultaneously and under the same aspect. We have the point of departure identified with the point of arrival. We have the beginning identified with the ending. As Whitehead would put it, we have the 'initial phase' identified with the 'satisfaction.' But so to identify the prior state with the latter state, to identify loss and gain, reduces itself to a contradiction.

If we have loss and gain separate, we must admit either (a) there is a lacuna in change, that is to say, there is a sudden leap from the point of departure to the point of arrival. Loss suddenly, and without continuity, becomes gain. (From the same point of view, of course.) But this is contrary to all natural, scientific, and philosophical experience and reasoning. As the philosopher says, "Natura non fit per saltum." Or we have to say (b) loss and gain reside in something stable which changes, which is our notion of substance, namely, a principle of stability within the entity, a

---

[11] Aristotle, *Met. XI*, 6 ; 1063 a 18; *In XI Met.* Lect. 6, No. 2234.

principle whereby the entity is due to be what it is. To go back to the identification of loss and gain. It may be said that they are two aspects of the same thing. If that is so, then there must exist some thing of which they are the two aspects. In summary, we have to explain change either by postulating some existing thing in potency to change, something which is capable of gaining or losing, or we have to eliminate change as a contradiction.

It is true that atomic physics may show that everything seems to be change, and change seems to be the reality of the universe. But we are speaking of metaphysical principles, principles that explain both change and the orderliness in change. These principles are being and becoming as explained by potency and act. Things are what they are because they are in act, and are limited by their capacities or potencies. They change because they have the capacities or potencies to exist, and to lose or receive perfections. Being which is limited is limited by potency, and because it is so limited, or contingent, because it can not-be, it is changeable. On the other hand, change itself means nothing without something that changes. Change may be said to be, as St. Thomas calls it, imperfect act. We may summarize this notion of being and becoming in the following statements:

1. Reality consists of being and becoming.[12]
2. All beings except God are limited by their potencies.[13]
3. The contingency of being necessitates change and causality.
4. Change supposes contingent being, being composed of potency and act.
5. Being is adequately divided by potency and act, both in reference to its participation in existence and in reference to the further perfections it may and does receive.
6. Being is that which exists in the order of actuality; becoming is the transition from one state to another.

Before passing to a critique of Whitehead's notions of being and becoming, there remains to consider, briefly, what we mean by substance. We have already seen that substance is not an inert substratum.[14] The whole Thomistic tradition of being and becoming as well as all of experience are opposed to such an explanation.

---

[12] Aristotle, *Met. XI*, 6; 1063 a 18; *In XI Met.*, Lect. 6, No. 2243.
[13] *S.T.*, P. 1a, Q. 25, A. 1-6; cf. *C.G.*, L. II, c. 15.
[14] *De Ente et Essentia.* C. I.

For the Thomist, substance is a principle of identity within the thing. We have seen that in change there is a fluid element and a stable element. The stable element is the principle of identity within the entity, that metaphysical principle of identity wherein a thing remains what it is despite the changes that it undergoes. That is what we mean by substance, not an inert substratum. Substance is that principle whereby a thing is due to exist in its own right.[15] It is opposed to accident, which is that which is due to inhere in another as in a subject, and which refers to those changing and additional perfections that inhere in a substance. The accidents are quality, quantity, relation, action, reception of action (passio), and various dispositions which go with the other accidents. Accidents are the properties and operations of the thing.

Substance is, as we have seen, limited. Corporeal substance, bodily substance, is composed of a determinable element and a determining element.[16] The former we call matter. We must note that for the Thomist, matter does not primarily mean the physically quantitative stuff that goes into the composition of the 'material' bodies. It is the potential, determinable element in bodies. The determining element we call form. We must remember that by form we do not mean shape. Form transcends shape, which latter, since it intrinsically inheres in quantity and quality, is accidental. Form is that principle which so unites with the potential element as to determine the composite into a specific capacity for existence. Hence, substance is that which is apt to exist in its own right, a principle of so existing, and a principle of identity within the entity. Form is the determining element in substance. Matter is the determinable element. Once again, these are the application of metaphysical principles to explain physical composition.

Matter and form are applications of potency and act. Matter, insofar as it is determinable, is potency. Form, insofar as it is determining, a principle of action, is act. Quantitative accidents, are rooted in matter, qualitative accidents in form. The operations of a thing are according to its nature, since it is the same form that determines a thing to be what it is, and determines the operations (or qualitative accidents) of that thing. We can summarize this notion of substance, form, and matter as follows:

---

[15] *In II Sent.*, D. 3, Q. 1, A. 1.
[16] *St. Thos.*, Opusc., *De Principiis Naturae.*

Critique of Whitehead's Theory of Being and Becoming

1. Substance is that which is apt to exist in its own right; a principle of identity within the thing.
2. Accidents are those perfections which are apt to exist in a substance.
3. Form is, primarily, the determining element in the thing, and secondarily, the root of qualitative accidents.
4. Matter is, primarily, the determinable element in the thing, and secondarily, the root of the quantitative accidents.

Having seen the above exposé of the Thomistic interpretation of reality, let us try to ascertain Whitehead's position. Can we say that he is a monist, or must we say that he is a pluralist? What are we to say about his 'actual occasions,' those units of reality all operating according to the ultimate, 'creativity?' We must review Whitehead's composite picture of reality.

Reality is process. It is the fusion of pure activity, the world of actual occasions, with the world of forms, 'eternal objects.' These passive forms enter into the activity that meets them. The meeting is constantly occurring. The two streams are constantly meeting, and according to the projection of the vector character into this reality, these two streams take a new direction, which is the unified stream of reality. The meeting of activity with any eternal object is the birth of a new actual occasion. Thus, since the nature of an actual event is the growing together into a new unity activity with a form, it is literally a 'concrescence.' At the first juncture of activity with an eternal object, the new event receives its initial aim, that is to say, its self-determined vector line. From then on, by its own activity, it follows the vector line, filling up its nature, organization, and direction to its self exhaustion in its satisfaction and objective immortality. Thus, each thing is a fusion, a union of activity with form, a self-perfecting. All is this endless process, as wide as reality. It is all a vast organic unity of relativity.[17]

The guiding principle *in* it, and the supreme example *in* it is the reason that guides it, God. God perfects Himself, since He is the wealth of potentialities (passive potentialities). He is the end of activity, since activity tends to unity with the eternal objects. He is deficient in actuality. As the process goes on in and through his guidance, He enriches himself. Thus, He is the supreme example of process.

---
[17] Cf. *Process and Reality*, p. 31 ff.

We must note how Whitehead's philosophy is the contrary of Thomism. For Whitehead, the determinable element is active and the determining element passive. For Whitehead, reality is a fusion of two principles into one principle. On the other hand, for Thomism, the determining delement is active and the determinable element passive. For Thomism, the basic problem of the one and the many is primarily one of the differentiation of being, instead of the fusion of activity.

Is Whitehead's philosophy monistic? We must answer in the affirmative. It may be urged that he supposes two principles, activity and eternal objects. Yet, he maintains only one intrinsic principle, namely, activity. All other principles are external.

It is a philosophy to erect a dynamistic interpretation of all reality while safeguarding the obvious manifestation of stability. Does it serve its purpose? Let us investigate its formal constitution to see if it can be maintained.

We may say, first of all, that the immediate weakness from which flows the general weakness is the actual entity. The fundamental unit of activity is the actual entity. In the 'ontological principle' it is declared to be the sufficient reason of all reality.[18] But the actual entity is activity, a growing together, subsistent activity. This, we have seen, is a contradiction. By the very fact that Whitehead supposes an extrinsic principle, the eternal object, to explain stability shows that the principle of sufficient reason is insufficient. It does not have the full reason of its existence within its essence. If the foundation is insufficient, what may we expect of the entire structure? Let us follow this weakness through the entire philosophy of reality.

Reality consists of the world of activity which meets the eternal objects. The active phase, the world of activity, is what we shall consider now; then we pass on to a consideration of the other phases. This active phase, we must say, is either (i) pure becoming, or (ii) not pure becoming, that is to say, being which becomes. If it is pure becoming, it is a contradiction, for as we have seen, and as we shall see repeated in the next chapter, pure becoming without a subject is a contradiction. Hence, if this active phase really exists, if it is really subsistent, it must be being which becomes. If it is really subsistent, it must be substance, which as we have

---

[18] *Process and Reality*, p. 28; cf. pp. 36, 37.

Critique of Whitehead's Theory of Being and Becoming 121

seen is 'that which is apt to exist in itself and not in another.' Hence, the active phase leads to substance. (The proof for these statements is to be found earlier in this chapter, in the exposition of Thomism on being and becoming. The rest of this chapter is but an application of Thomism to the philosophy of Whitehead.)

As for the eternal objects, we may apply the same dilemma. If these eternal objects really enter into the composition of actual events, they must really exist. If they really exist, somewhat after the manner of Plato's separated forms, they are either (i) pure becoming, which we have seen to be a contradiction, or they are (ii) not pure becoming, that is to say they are beings. If they are beings, they either subsist or do not subsist. If they subsist, they must be substances. If they do not subsist, they must exist in something else either as (a) ideas—in which case they cannot enter into the real composition of real actual events— or (b) as extra-mental accidents. In either event, their essence is to exist in something else as in a subject. But the subject must subsist, and hence we are led again to substance.

So far, then, the active component of actual events must lead to substance, and has no explanation without substance. Similarly, the eternal objects lead to substance and have no explanation without it. Now, what of the union of the two?

The composing principles are either complete or incomplete. If they are complete principles, then the union of activity with eternal objects is only an accidental union. If that is true, Whitehead can in no way say that all entities are the same, actual events, differing only in organization according to high-grade and low-grade societies. If the composing principles are incomplete, then Whitehead's theory becomes an accidentally monistic theory which is really substantial in reality, for if the principles are incomplete and are ordained in their very natures for union (as the Thomist would say, 'transcendentally related'), then Whitehead must fall back upon the Thomistic notion of substance composed of two *intrinsic* principles in physical entities.

Thus we may, for the time, conclude that if Whitehead wishes to maintain his theory of union of activity with eternal objects, he must arrive at substance somewhere along the line of his proof. However, we must note that Whitehead, in professedly rejecting substance, is correct in rejecting the connotation of substance to which he is opposed. Whitehead is opposed to the Lockian and

Spinozan notions of substance. For Locke, substance is an inert substratum physically upholding those characteristics and operations that we call accidents. Such a notion is also rejected by the Thomist because an inert substratum cannot be a principle of activity.[19] Descartes' notion of substance, as well as that of Spinoza, is that which exists *by* itself. The scholastic rejects that notion because it makes each and every thing absolutely necessary, denies change, otherness, causality. Whitehead is not correct in attributing these notions of substance to Thomism. The notion of substance that we maintain must be held by Whitehead is the proper Thomistic notion, namely, 'that whose nature is to exist *in* itself and not in another.' This notion denies neither the interrelation of entities, their differentiation, their being caused, their contingency. It also guards and maintains a certain measure of subsistence.

Let us now consider Whitehead's theory from another point of view, still maintaining our investigation from the formal constitution of the actual entity. Suppose it be urged that this union of activity and eternal objects be only a logical (instead of an ontological) explanation of what is in itself manifestitative of an active phase and a stable phase. Since these events subsist, we must arrive at the conclusion that they are either pure becoming (again, a contradiction) or beings which become, that is to say, substance. The second alternative leads to the question of the possibility of passive forms.

We must first note that the word 'form' is a label, a term expressive of the essence of a thing. The term *follows* the nature of the thing. We first discover the necessity of a determining principle and then give it the term 'form.' We do *not* formulate the term, and then erect a philosophy to fit the term. We do not beg the question by supposing what we wish to prove. This we must keep in mind.

In keeping with experience, we see things specifically diverse. We know of the specific diversity from specifically diverse operations. Since the operations themselves are specifically diverse, they must flow from specifically diverse principles, and they must flow from active principles. After all, the source of activity must be active or else we maintain the unscientific and unphilosophic tenet

---

[19] *De Ente et Essentia*, C. 1.

Critique of Whitehead's Theory of Being and Becoming

that more can be obtained from less. Were these activities identical, we would have to postulate only one principle of activity. Since they are diverse, in each atom, each molecule, each element, we must maintain an active principle of specific determination. This we call form.

Furthermore, form must be an intrinsic principle. Operations come from within. Otherwise we would have subsistent operation, which is the equivalent of pure becoming, a contradiction. Hence, in each entity, there must be an intrinsic determining active principle. The specification of anything, the determining of anything, is active. Hence, the form from which it flows must be active. To maintain that the form is passive is to say that the source of activity in anything is passive, which ultimately reduces itself to a contradiction, and which does not give the sufficient reason of a thing's activity.

Let us see the consequences of rejecting this explanation. The eternal objects, the passive forms, are either intrinsic or extrinsic. If they are intrinsic, they are passive principles of activity. If they are extrinsic, to be truly guides of process in the development of actual events they must be active. Yet Whitehead has called them 'pure potentialities.' Furthermore, if they are extrinsic they are only accidental guides, leaving the only reality to be subsistent intrinsic change.

But here is the greatest indictment against extrinsic forms, whether active or passive. If activity is guided by extrinsic forms, it must have within itself the intrinsic principle to be guided. If eternal objects can enter into activity, this activity must have the intrinsic capacity to receive the eternal objects. Thus, in order that an actual occasion be what it is, it must also have within itself the passive principle to receive external activity. Hence, in its nature, it is not only active, but passive as well, and to explain the differentiation, stability, and development of changing things, we must postulate not only intrinsically active forms, but also an intrinsic principle of limitation. This is scarcely consonant with a monistic philosophy. Yet it is necessitated by such a philosophy, showing that monism is scarcely the answer.

Now let us change our viewpoint from the formal constitution of the components of the actual entity to the viewpoint of efficiency and finality in relation to Whitehead's explanation of reality. In

124 The Philosophy of Being of Alfred North Whitehead

other words, let us apply the questions "Whence?" and "Where?" to Whitehead's system.

We have seen that Whitehead postulates subsistent activity and subsistent forms, or eternal objects, which, we must remember, are pure potentials. Now, we can say three things about these: (i) the forms and activity enter into composition and produce actual events. This, we have seen, supposes substance on the part of the activity and the potentials. (And we must remember that determining potentials are a contradiction.) (ii) The only reality is the activity; the eternal objects are only ideas. To this we must say that ideas do not guide activity physically save through a physical agent. This, even granting subsistent activity, which we have seen allows for neither causation nor differentiation, and which is a contradiction unless we have subsistent substances which act. (iii) The eternal objects exist in God and all the activity takes place in God. Concerning the untenability of this explanation we shall investigate in the last chapter on the critique of Whitehead's explanation of God.

To each of these three alternatives we must apply the principles of sufficient reason and efficient causality to ask the questions? "Whence do this activity and these eternal objects come? What is the sufficient reason of their being?" We cannot say that they are explicable in themselves. They are tending towards further perfections, and by that fact do not have the explanation of their existence in their essences. They are limited, and yet they gain new perfections. Hence they must find a reason for existence outside of themselves. Whitehead does not explain what this principle is. He speaks of God as the directing agent and directing reason for the ingression of new forms into activity, but God Himself is part of the process, and hence is no explanation of the process. Since there is no external explanation, there is the difficulty of getting more from less. Activity and eternal objects are potentially actual events. What is the principle that actualizes these potentialities? Whitehead does not answer that question, but speaks of self-causation. As we shall see in the next chapter, even though potency is in itself a real capacity, this real capacity cannot reduce itself to actuality, because potency in relation to its act is a definite lack of its act, is deficient in its act, is, we may say, a relative nothing. Something greater does not come from something less. This is a basic law of human reasoning, and to deny it is to deny all science, all knowledge, and consequently, all reality. Hence, to neglect to explain where creativity and eternal objects come from, what may be their cause (since, insofar as the reason of their existence is not identical with their existence they demand a cause) is a serious deficiency in Whitehead's philosophy.

There is a similar deficiency in regard to the final cause of all reality. What is it all for? What is its purpose? Is it creativity for the sake of creativity? Process itself has no meaning unless it is either (i) for the attaining of some being (for process is a tendency, and a tendency means a tending for something, the reduction from potency to act. To deny this is to stumble into an infinite series of process for process for process ad infinitum.); or (ii) the operation of some being. Just as a tendency *to* a tendency is not in itself explicable, neither is a tendency *from* a tendency in itself explicable. The basic reason for this is that, as we have seen, no potency can reduce itself from potency to act. And process, or tendency, or creativity, is the reduction from one state to another, from *some thing* in potency to *some thing* in act. St. Thomas has a much more satisfying answer when he says that all things operate for one end, God. Whitehead has no such satisfying answer, for he makes God part of the process, and hence has process for the sake of process.

Having investigated Whitehead's theory of being and becoming from the point of view of its formal constitution, as well as from the point of view of efficient and final causality, we must come to the conclusion that his philosophy is untenable because of his denial of substance, of being. Every phase of his philosophy, every tenet of his metaphysics is based upon, or rather, has no meaning without the Thomistic notion of substance. Whitehead is philosophizing in the first and second degrees of abstraction. But those degrees of abstraction are limited according to the limitations of natural science and mathematics. They only allow a man to stop at change and relation.

There remain two problems. In comparison with modern atomic physics, who is right? Whitehead or ourselves? Whitehead would probably tell us that it is impossible to hold any notion of being and substance because of the data of modern physics. After all, even in what we consider the most stable of things we know there is amazing molecular and atomic energy between atoms and among the components of the atom. We willingly grant that *physically* all things consist of molecules and atoms, and that atoms further consist of protons, neutrons, electrons, positrons, and whatever other units there may be in the atom. But we add that the order of existence of all things, depending as it does on the order of operation of these units, depends upon a pattern of arrangement of these units. The hydrogen atom remains a hydrogen atom, the radium atom a radium atom, the uranium atom a uranium atom because of the patterned arrangement of the compoent units. Why do these things exist and act in their definite patterns? Why do they not go off in a tangent, run amuck? Why is there not chaos instead of order? In other words, why is there this order among them, this order that gives the physical explanation of order throughout the entire universe?

The answer is that there must be a principle whereby they exist and whereby they operate as they do. In other words, there must be a principle of identity within the atom itself, and a principle whereby it subsists as the atom that it is. This we call substance, and we see no repugnance between the physical explanation of the universe and the metaphysical explanation of substance. On the contrary, we welcome the physical, atomic, explanation since it is a further proof of our doctrine of substance. (We may also note that the transmutation caused by the stripping of atoms of their particles is possible only because of this intrinsic principle which makes them what they are.)

The second remaining problem is that of Whitehead's relativism. Relativism, we maintain, supposes substance. Whitehead has a great deal of relativism in *Process and Reality*. He summarizes it simply[20] in a brief work, one of his last written works, entitled *Immortality*. He postulates relativity against the Cartesian definition of substance, namely, 'that which needs nothing other than itself to exist.' Thus he says:

> "This answer involves complete disagreement with a widespread tradition of philosophic thought. This erroneous tradition presupposes independent existences. . . .[21]

Of course, independent existences have no place in a philosophy of organism, where interdependence is stressed. Whitehead gives a number of examples wherein we must weigh every statement to

---
[20] *Immortality*, in the Anthology, *The Philosophy of Alfred North Whitehead;* p. 698 ff.
[21] *Ibid.*, p. 698.

realize that there are no universal statements, for every statement depends upon the circumstances of the particular case. Thus, one and one make more than two if one unit is a spark and the other a keg of gunpowder. Hence the statement is not universal.

> "In fact, there is not a sentence, or a word, with a meaning which is independent of the circumstances under which it is uttered."[22]

Of course, we disagree with that statement for two reasons: (i) Whitehead is inveighing against a false notion of substance; and (ii) relativity presupposes substance.

For the first point. We have only to realize that which we have already seen of the Thomistic notion of substance. Substance is *not* that which exists *by* itself. It is that which, having depended upon other entities for its existence, exists *in* itself with a certain measure of subsistence. If each entity exists by itself, it would need nothing other than itself to exist. It would eliminate all causality. Such we know is not the case. This leads to the second point, namely, that relativity supposes substance.

We maintain, just as firmly as Whitehead, that each thing, existing as it does with a certain measure of subsistence, also exists with a great measure of dependence upon other things. Each and every created thing depends upon a cause, or several causes, for its beginning. It depends upon many things for its continued existence. We, too, maintain a world of interdependence. Examples of this are obvious. But, we also maintain that all this interdependence, the relations of so many entities one upon the other all suppose things which are related to one another. We have seen the necessity of substance, we have seen that activity has no meaning unless there is something active. Similarly, relation has no meaning unless it is between substances which are related. Whitehead argues against substance, because he seems to think that substance necessitates complete independence of each thing from the other. He seems to think that Scholasticism denies interdependence, whereas Scholasticism stoutly maintains interdependence, causality, and explains it not in terms of monism, but in terms of potency and act.

To deny that we can make exact statements which transcend time and space because of the interdependence of each thing upon

---

[22] *Immortality*, p. 699.

the other is not only superficial, but also leads to scepticism. After all, we can say that a man is a rational animal, always was such, and always will be such. We can make that statement despite the dependence of a man upon his parents for his beginning and despite such circumstances as food, climate, and employment for the continued subsistence of his being. Circumstances are accidental, whereas the nature of man partakes of subsistence insofar as man, in his nature, is what he is; because man is a substance. To go back to Whitehead's example of the spark and the gunpowder we may say that the real reason why the spark and the gunpowder will add up to two but will efficiently make more than two is because the spark is what it is and the gunpowder is what it is.

In conclusion, we may classify Whitehead's philosophy as dynamic monism. It is a system erected to interpret reality in terms of process. His ultimate, 'creativity,' is the great reality, the beginning and end of all things. It is his "Category of the Ultimate," and it "replaces Aristotle's category of 'primary substance.'"[23] His "Categories of Existence" are all activity in varied forms, namely, 'actual events,' 'prehensions,' 'concrescences.' The first of his "Categories of Explanation" is that:

". . . the actual world is a process, and that process is the becoming of actual entities."[24]

This is ordered through the 'ingression' of eternal objects into actual events. The dynamism is apparent throughout.

We may also note the interplay between dynamic monism and empiricism, as well as the interplay between the mathematically trained mind and the relativism intrinsic to the philosophy of organism. We may conclude by saying that the basic weakness in the philosophy of organism is the substitution of mathematical abstraction for metaphysical abstraction. Mathematical abstraction leads the mind along a particular line far removed from experience. In order to safeguard the validity of experience, in order to "endeavor to frame a coherent, logical, necessary system of general ideas in terms of which every element of our experience can be interpreted,"[25] Whitehead is forced to erect a bulky and vulnerable system, which, since it is open to attack on every side

[23] *Process and Reality*, p. 32.
[24] *Ibid.*, p. 33. Cf. also, pp. 31 ff.
[25] *Ibid.*, p. 4.

and weak in almost every postulate, does not serve the purpose for which it is ordained.

SUMMARY

This chapter is best summarized by the table proposed below:

	Whitehead	St. Thomas
Type of philosophy:	Dynamic monism	Substantial metaphysics (Moderate dualism)
Fundamental problem:	The One and the Many	The One and the Many
Fundamental unit of reality:	The actual entity	Individual substance
Explanation:	Through external forms; fusion of many univocal units of becoming into one reality of creativity	Through intrinsic principles of potency and act; differentiation of being, according to individual essences into many analogous beings
Intrinsic principle:	One—creativity	Two, potency and act (save in God)
The ultimate:	Creativity (process or becoming)	God as the Absolute Fulness of Being, Pure Act—no intrinsic composition
Manner of development:	Complicated; necessary forcing of theory to conform with experienced reality	Logical and simple; application of potency and act to all created reality
Characteristics:	Fails to give sufficient reason. If not reduced to substantial metaphysics, leads to contradictions on all basic postulates	Foundation and development based on principles of identity, non-contradiction, sufficient reason
	Inconsistent with reality	Consistent throughout

CHAPTER VIII

A Critique of Whitehead's Philosophy of Cause

The notion of causality seems universal in the thought of mankind. That does not mean that all will agree as to the true explanation of causality. For example, the empiricists admit the fact of the notion of causality. They admit that men have ideas of cause and effect. However, they try to explain it as a subjective state of mind. Still, they admit that people have a notion of cause and effect.

Thomistic philosophers maintain causality as a fundamental principle of reality. They hold that there is an objective order of things depending upon orderly objective causality. Here they are following both Aristotle and St. Thomas. Aristotle had given an account of how men seek wisdom in an orderly fashion, and had given examples of workers and artisans, doctors and patients, and had shown how men naturally seek a causal order in things.[1] Then he arrives at the conclusion that the proper object of the wise man is to seek "original causes."[2] St. Thomas, commenting upon this, remarks that Aristotle makes it evident that philosophy is the speculative wisdom of causes and that we must begin from the causes of things. In the *Summa Contra Gentiles* he begins by agreeing with Aristotle that wisdom is the consideration of ultimate causes.[3] Hence we see that in Thomistic philosophy, causality is intimately bound up with knowledge. Even the physical sciences maintain this attitude. The physicist, chemist, astronomer, biologist,—in fact, all who make a careful study of reality—are constantly asking the threefold question "What? How? Why?" This implicit recognition of causality leads into the further questions, "To what end can this be put?" That implicit belief in the use of means to an end, which in itself is another statement of causality, is the entire background of the great manufacturing companies which keep expensive laboratories for the perfection of their products.

---

[1] *Met. I*, 1 and 2.
[2] *Met. I*, 3; 983 a 24; cf. St. Thos., *In I Met.*, Lect. 3 and 4.
[3] *C. G.* 1, 1.

When Aristotle and St. Thomas use their examples of men making and causing things, when Aristotle shows how by a combination of induction and deduction we are led into a knowledge of principles and causes, they reiterate the fact that causality and the search for causes is a self-evident fact of human experience. Even children, when they begin to think, begin to ask for explanations of things in terms of causality. They are constantly asking "What, how, why?" We can summarize the entire philosophy of causality in those questions.

So much, then, for the recognition of the fact of causality. We must see the metaphysical explanation of cause in its relation to being and becoming. This we can take entirely from St. Thomas. In brief, it is, again, the analogy of being. Anything that exists will have the reason of its existence either in itself or not in itself. That is to say, its essence is to exist either in itself or not in itself. Its essence will either be *simply to exist* or *to participate in existence*. If its essence is to exist, then it will necessarily exist. It will have the reason of its existence in itself. It will be existent being univocally. It will be existent being necessarily. If it participates in existence, the reason of its existence will be outside of itself and in something else. It will depend upon that something else for the reason of its existence, and hence, for its actual existence. It will thus be contingent, depending upon something else for its beginning its coming into existence, as well as for its actual existence. Hence it will be caused. That is the necessity of cause. Essences exist potentially. To reduce them to actuality, something else which contains the reason of their existence is required.

The fact is that being is not univocal. If it were, if everything had within it the reason for its existence, there would be no change, no becoming, no causality, no passing away. Yet change, becoming, passing away, are the most common of phenomena. We have seen how subsistent change is a contradiction. The only answer left is being which becomes. But being which becomes is being through participation, being composed of potency and act, being the reason of whose existence is outside of itself, caused being. Thus it is that St. Thomas maintains that being through participation, composite being, requires a cause.[4] Thus it is that causality, in Thomism, is the metaphysical explanation of the becoming of

[4] *De Ente et Essentia*, C. V. Cf. *S.T.*, P. 1a, Q. 3, A. 4; Q. 3, A. 7; Q. 44, A. 1; *C.G.*, L. II, c. 15.

composite substance. It is the metaphysical reconciliation of being and becoming.

In tracing through causality as the metaphysical explanation of being and becoming in composite and contingent substances, we may say that created substances both depend upon and contribute to the being and becoming of other substances. In the analogy of being, St. Thomas and the Thomists maintain as stoutly as Whitehead that change is one of the most common of phenomena. Change is the difference between God and created being.[5] However, as we have seen, the Thomists do not confound or identify the two. The Thomistic position is that substance changes, not that substance is change.[6] Thomists maintain that in all change there is a subject which changes. Here they follow Aristotle.[7]

What is the principle of change in the contingent substance? The principle that guarantees differentiation and causation? The Scholastic answer is potency and act, capacity and actuality. Whenever a being changes, it passes from potency to act. Whatever exists must be possible. Whatever gains a perfection must have the capacity for that perfection. All being that changes passes from potency to act, insofar as in change it is always gaining something, which in itself is the gaining of a perfection. That is what is meant by the process of action, and action, according to St. Thomas, is the actualization of an active potency.[8]

In relation to its act, or the perfection sought, a potency is a privation, or a relative nothing. And since from nothing nothing comes, in the case of relative nothing, there must be something to supply the deficient activity. Hence, there must be act. (We must also here remember that any being, insofar as it is a being, and therefore in a certain grade of perfection, is in act.) But, since potency is not in the act to which it is ordained, there must be another act to reduce it to act. That other such must be a being, since as we have seen, pure becoming without a subject which becomes is a contradiction, and a contradiction is nothing. That is why Aristotle makes it a fundamental principle that whatever is moved is moved by another.[9] That is also why St. Thomas,

---

[5] *S.T.*, P. 1, Q. 2, A. 3.
[6] *S.T.*, P. 1, Q. 45, A. 3c; *In XI Met.*, lect. 6, No. 2234, 2243.
[7] *Met.* XI, 6; 1063a 18.
[8] *S.T.* P. 1a, Q. 54, A. 1c; *C.G.* L. II, c. 9.
[9] *Physics*, Book II, Book III, Book VII, 1; 241b, 24 ff.

applying potency and act to all created being, states that it is a contradiction for a thing to change itself. To say that a thing reduces itself from potency to act is to say that a thing is both act and non-act simultaneously and in the same respect.[10]

That is the Principle of Efficient Causality, namely, that what is moved is moved by another. Jacques Maritain, in keeping with the spirit of St. Thomas, prefers as the Principle of Causality, "Nihil reducit se de potentia in actum"[11] as the full metaphysical character of the necessity of being for causality, and the necessity for being to bring about the existence and changes in another. It is another way of saying that if a thing does not have the sufficient reason of its being and existence in itself, it must have that reason in another.

However, and here we are anticipating somewhat, we must note that efficient causality is not the only cause based upon the relation of potency to act. All causality is based upon that. Material cause is cause simply because matter has the potency to receive a certain form. Formal causality is based upon potency and act because it is an act that realizes the potencies of matter. Final cause is similarly based because it is an act towards which beings, through their potencies, can tend. Thus it is that efficiency, finality, formality, and materiality are all, insofar as they are causes, part of the link between being and becoming.

Before passing on to the definition and division of causes, we can summarize the metaphysical character of cause as follows: (i) every contingent being postulates a cause as the reason for its existence; (ii) the reduction of potency to act requires a cause, for to say that a thing can reduce itself from potency to act is to state a contradiction; (iii) cause can only be a subsistent substance, for subsistent becoming is a contradiction.

Concerning the nature of cause, Thomists, following St. Thomas, go much further than Aristotle. As far as we know, Aristotle had failed to formulate the exact distinction between principle and cause. He had said that "causes are spoken of in an equal number of senses: for all causes are beginnings (principles)."[12] However, we do not find him stating that all principles are not causes. Furthermore, he sets out almost immediately to describe the four

---

[10] *S.T.* P. 1a, Q. 2, A. 3c.
[11] *Preface to Metaphysics*, p. 136.
[12] *Met. IV*, 1; 1013a 17.

causes without (again, as far as we know) giving a strict definition of cause as such.

We may define cause as:

> "That particular species of principle, which, by positive influx, contributes being to, or contributes to the being or becoming of something distinct from itself and on which that other is dependent in the measure of its contribution."[13]

This definition, based as it is upon St. Thomas's professed statements about the nature of cause,[14] admirably summarizes all that we have said before concerning the necessity of cause, namely, that every contingent being (that is, a being not having the reason of its existence as its essence) depends upon the extrinsic being that has the reason of its (the effect's) being. Hence, in the nature of cause according to St. Thomas, we find the following elements: (i) a positive contribution (thus eliminating mere sequential precedence, or those things that go into the removal of obstacles); (ii) to the being or becoming of a distinct thing; (iii) entailing dependence of effect upon cause.

What, then, are the causes that fulfill the Thomistic definition and conditions of cause? Aristotle lists four[15] and in this he is followed by St. Thomas and the scholastics.[16] These four are the material, formal, efficient, and final causes. The material and formal causes enter into the composition of the thing. The efficient cause is the agent bringing about the new entity, while the final cause is the reason why the new entity is brought into being.

In particular, first, concerning material cause, we may say that St. Thomas adopts Aristotle's notion and explanation of material cause almost without change. Aristotle had defined it as:

> "... the primary substratum of each thing, from which it comes to be without qualification and which persists in the result."[17]

St. Thomas is a bit more specific in his definition, which is:

---

[13] Meehan, F.X., *Efficient Causality in St. Thomas*, p. 174.
[14] Cf. *In V Met.* I #751; *In I Sent.* 29, 1, 1c; *In I Phys.* 1; *S.T.* P. 1a, Q. 33 A. 1c; *In V Met.* I, #750.
[15] *Met.* 1, 3; 983a 24; *Phys.* 2, 3; 194 23 ff.
[16] *C.G.* 3, 10; cf. *S.T.* P. 1a, Q. 3, A. 8c; *Opusc.* #31 *De Principiis Naturae*.
[17] *Phys.* I, 9; 192a 31.

"... that out of which something is made, and which is 'existing-in', that is, existing within."[18]

That last phrase 'intus existens' differentiates immediately from efficient and final cause, which are outside of the thing. Hence material cause is that out of which something becomes. Prime matter does not exist as such. It exists in things already informed as a potency for being made into a new substance. However by the fact that it exists in substances already informed, it is already predisposed to be made into certain—not any or all—other substances. As Aristotle says:

> "Regarding material substances we must not forget that even if all things come from the same first cause or have the same things for their first causes, and if yet the same matter serves as a starting point for their generation, yet there is a matter proper for each. . . ."[19]

He gives a number of examples of this, e.g., a bed and a chest may be made from wood. "But some different things must have their matter different; e.g., a saw could not be made from wood. . . ."[20] Thus although prime matter may be considered pure potency for any information, as a matter of fact, matter, since it is already informed, is predisposed only to certain other informations. That, of course, depends upon the form it already has.

The exact causality of matter is to give itself as a positive production to the formation of a new entity. In this way it fulfills the definition of cause.

The principle of determination in the production of a new being is the 'formal cause.' This is what St. Thomas calls the 'forma secundum quam,'[21] and is the principle whereby a thing is made what it is. Form is either educed from the potencies of matter or it enters into a substantial union with matter (the latter in the case of 'subsistent forms'—i.e. those forms which can exist separated from matter). The two, matter and form, become the substance of the new being. It is the principle that determines a thing into a determined species of being. In this, form differs from the 'accidental form,' which adds some accidental perfection to an already determined substance.[22] The substantial form, inso-

---

[18] *In V Met.*, II #763. The translation into English is my own.
[19] *Met. VII*, 4; 1044a 15 ff.
[20] *Ibid.*, 27 ff.
[21] *Qq. Dd. De Verit.*, Q. 3, A. 1c.
[22] *Qq. Dd. De Spirit. Creat.*, A. 1, 9.

far as it realizes the possibility or potency of a thing to become something new, is related to matter as act to potency. The form is the act of the matter.

Form has a twofold function. The primary function is the information of matter. That is its prime purpose insofar as it is a determinant of substance. Its secondary purpose is to be source of operation. Because both determination of substance and operations proceed from form as from a principle, since both proceed from the same form, we are guaranteed the truth of the Thomistic dictum 'operatio sequitur esse,' which dictum assures the possibility of our knowing the natures of things a posteriori. This is of prime importance for the attainment of truth.

Closely allied to the formal cause is the exemplary cause, which St. Thomas calls the 'forma ad quam.'[23] This is also called the formal extrinsic cause. It has its real place in causality because it helps to the determination of a new being. It is the exemplar, or type, according to which a thing is made. However, it is not usually considered a separate cause, since it has its relations with the formal, efficient, and final causes.

As the type, it is related to those causes as follows: (i) to the formal cause, as the extrinsic correspondent of the form which is to inform the new being; (ii) to the efficient cause, as the exemplar guiding the efficient cause's effecting the information of the new being; (iii) to the final cause, as the archtype, the imitation of which is intended.

The efficient cause is called by St. Thomas the 'forma a qua,' and has for its characteristic note causality by activity or action. Aristotle had defined efficient cause as that cause "Whence is the first beginning of change or of rest."[24] St. Thomas, on the whole, follows him in this definition[25] but does not limit action to successive motion. He states ex professo that creation is causality,[26] and in creation there is no succession, since there is no terminus a quo. However, creation fulfills the definition of efficient causality, namely, positive production of a new being (or new beings) through activity.

---

[23] *Qq. Dd. De Verit.*, Q. 3, A. 1c.
[24] *Met. IV*, 2; 1013a 29.
[25] *In V Met.* Lect. 2, #756.
[26] *S.T.* P. 1a, Q. 45, A. 6c.

The main point about efficient causality is the fact that its mode of causality is action, which, as we have seen, is the actualization of an active potency. By action, the efficient cause unites matter and form, reducing the form as the act of a potency in being. This philosophical explanation is tested and confirmed by experience. Men are constantly making things and doing things by action. The philosophical necessity depends upon the fact that no being can reduce itself from potency to act. This is one of St. Thomas's great proofs for the existence of God.[27]

Final cause, for both Aristotle and St. Thomas, is that for the sake of which something is done, that on account of whose appetibility the agent acts.[28] It, too, is based upon the fact that things consist of potency and act, that things thus change, and that in changing they are acting for a good, a perfection. The end is the good or satisfaction that attracts. The quest for the good is related to efficiency, for the final cause is that which attracts, whereas the efficient cause is that principle which brings about the good by its action. That is the philosophical necessity and causality of final cause, namely, bringing things into being by attraction, which attraction sets efficient causality into action. It is well summarized by St. Thomas as follows:

> "Thus, then, he (Aristotle) indicates three things through final cause: namely, that it is the terminal of motion, and in this way is opposed to the principle of motion, which is efficient cause; and that it is first in intention, by reason of which it is said to be the cause of this; and that it is in itself appetible, by reason of which it is said to be good. For good is that which all things seek. Hence, showing in what manner final cause is opposed to efficient cause, he says that it is the end of generation and change, of which efficient cause is the principle."[29]

Here we must notice that final cause is the end of all things, setting the efficient cause into uniting matter and form; that it is the first in intention, therefore the reason or purpose in causality; because it is good, and therefore desirable. That is its causality, namely, that by attraction it contributes to the positive production of being. It is the beginning and end of causality, for it is first in intention, and last in execution.

---

[27] *S.T.* P. la, Q. 2, A. 3c.
[28] *Met. I*, 3; 983a 31; cf. *In I Met.* IV #71.
[29] *In I Met.*, IV #71. The translation into English is my own.

The importance of final cause is found in its attraction. It is the cause of causes. Efficient causes do not make ends, they are attracted to them. Thus, in attracting efficient cause, it brings about the union of matter and form. Hence, in that way, it is the cause of efficient, formal, causes. We might also say that the reason why formal causes and material cause are compatible is their ordination to tend to certain other things. Yet, in a sense, efficient cause may be said to be the cause of final cause, since it brings about beings, which is turn, because of their goodness, attract other beings.

Final cause, in rational natures, attracts through the recognition of and volition of goods. In non-rational natures, it attracts through natural tendencies. For example, the plant root has a natural tendency for water and certain minerals. The birds have an instinctive tendency to build nests in a certain way.[30]

Thus we can see the importance of final cause, since it is the cause of the other causes, since it, too, is explanatory of change, and since it implies a teleology in all created being.

We might summarize the Thomistic explanation of causality in the following way:

1. It is based upon potency and act, necessitated by 'being through participation.' It is a simple explanation, for it is clearly explanatory of what men know and do.

2. It is adequate, for it explains what things are, namely, a union of matter and differentiating form. This accounts, in a simple manner, for similarities and differences in all things. It explains how things come into being, and into a specific grade of being, through explaining that efficient cause unites matter and form as the transition from potency and act. It explains why things are what they are, by showing that all things act for a purpose. This is final cause. All of this is based upon the reduction from potency to act, and ultimately, upon the principles of sufficient reason and identity.

3. It is the simple link between being and becoming. In the principle of causality, we realize that to explain becoming we must have being. To explain the divergencies and natures of being, we must have becoming. Thomistic causality explains—once again,

---

[30] Cf. *Phys.* II, 8; 199a 20, where Aristotle gives a number of examples of teleology in non-rational beings.

completely confirmed by human experience—how beings bring about the perfection of other beings through causality.

Granted the obvious fact that things are and things change, the Thomistic doctrine of causality is a simple, obvious, and thoroughly scientific as well as thoroughly adequate explanation of that fact.

And now, in making a comparison with Whitehead's philosophy of cause, we must note first of all that as regards the *fact* of causality, Whitehead comes close to the Thomistic notion of causality. Many things which he postulates, especially as regards final cause as self-perfection, strike a note familiar to Thomism. That is because for both Whitehead and Thomists, the ultimate test of causality is experience.

It is concerning the nature of causality and the functions of the various causes that we find the difference. That is based upon the differences between Whitehead's philosophy of organism and the Thomistic explanation of reality. We must remember that for Whitehead, all is process; being is becoming, and to define a thing is to define its concrescences and processes. The Thomistic notion of change, of being and becoming, is that of beings which become and which change. For the Thomist, becoming is not synonymous with being. The two are not univocal, although they are necessarily connected, in contingent being, for all beings come to be, change, and pass away,—all beings except God.

Logically, Whitehead should not hold causality. His philosophy is monistic, and unless a monistic philosophy is inconsistent with its principles, it has place neither for differentiation nor for causality. Then again, causality, explanatory as it is of change in relation to being through the reduction from potency to act, implies being that is in act. If we say that all is change, we must imply not-becoming, for change as constant flux means that there is continuous gain and loss. Gain is becoming and loss may be considered as non-becoming. If a thing *is* becoming, due to the constant gain and loss that it *is*, we are led to the conclusion that a thing is, in its nature and simultaneously, non-becoming. That is another aspect of the reduction of subsistent becoming to a contradiction. If we say that a thing is a being which becomes, then we guarantee becoming, differentiation, causality, reality as it is and as it is experienced.

Now for Whitehead's causality in particular. We can consider

(i) final cause and self-causation; (ii) efficient cause; (iii) formal cause.

1. *Final Cause.* Final cause, for Whitehead, is the principle of unrest, namely, the constant quest for self-causation, the principle of self-causation. This is advanced through feelings, whereby the subject feels, following lures in its selection of the means that will help in the attainment of satisfaction. This process of self-causation is the source of activity, the matrix of form, the self-sufficiency or autonomy of everything. It is the reason why a thing is its own reason. It receives its initial phase from God and draws upon other actual entities for what we might call its substantial phase.

2. *Efficient Cause.* Efficient cause, as we have seen, is the counterpart or co-worker with final cause for the self-perfection of new entities. It is the auxiliary of final cause. It takes place in those entities that have reached satisfaction, and presupposes that the efficient cause has already reached the point of self-causation. The activity of the efficient cause is to offer its activity as data for the final cause. If the data is accepted, it is efficient cause. It does not correlate matter and form. It is merely acceptable or not acceptable to the entity that is going through the process of self-causation. However, if acceptable, by its activity it helps the final cause in the process of self-causation.

3. *Formal Cause.* This is the mode of operation of an entity in the process of self-causation. Consequent to the ingression of the eternal object into the actual entity, it is the principle guiding the choice of data in the feelings which work together in final and efficient causation. It is an extrinsic potency actualized by the subject into which it enters, instead of an intrinsic principle educed from or induced into an intrinsic potency by an extrinsic agent.

Strictly speaking, there is no such thing as material cause in the philosophy of organism. There is no substance as we know it, also no matter. There are, however, potentials out of which other things are made, namely, those actual entities which have arrived at the state of satisfaction.

In general, causality par excellence is the interwork of final and efficient cause. Of these two, final cause is *the* cause, since upon it depends the causality of self-causation, since it is intrinsically connected with the world of eternal objects. Final and efficient causes are fundamental in the philosophy of Whitehead. They are intrinsically connected with his 'ontological principle.'

"... This category of explanation is termed the 'ontological principle.' It could also be termed the 'principle of efficient, and final, causation ..."[31]

In a critical consideration of Whitehead's understanding and presentation of the causes, we can say the following:

1. *Final Cause.* There is much in what Whitehead says with which we can agree. Self-perfection is always to be considered an end according to Thomism. A being naturally acts with self-perfection as one of its ends. Furthermore, the use of means to reach that end of self-perfection is another norm of final cause. Means themselves, as goods, can be considered intermediate ends. Again, the existence of tendencies in natural feelings and tropisms is thoroughly scholastic, for it is only in the intellectual order that we find conscious teleology. In the non-conscious order, teleology is found in the natural tendencies of things. Then again, if finality works by attraction (as Whitehead sometimes seems to imply) another condition of final cause according to Scholasticism is fulfilled. Also, it is quite true to say that a being, or entity, gets its initial phase from God through exemplars, for according to Thomism, it is God Who is the ultimate source of teleology.

However, in disagreement, we may note the following points. Even though Whitehead sometimes seems to imply that final cause works through attraction, his doctrine of self-causation implies a contradiction, for no potency can reduce itself to act. It also implies a great deal of activity in self-causation. Yet, final cause is a good to be sought by other causes. The end does not reach itself. It is reached.

Whitehead also has a tendency to confuse final cause with formal cause. It is form, according to Thomism, that is the source of activity in a being. It is the form that determines the nature of the thing.

Furthermore, the place where Whitehead's finality is weak is in its inadequacy. Whitehead postulates that God is not an exception to metaphysics, and in that we agree. According to Whitehead, then, God is His Own End. Again, we agree. But if Whitehead is consistent, he must state that God has an initial phase. In fact,

---

[31] *Process and Reality*, p. 36.

he implies that, for he speaks at great length of the 'primordial nature' of God. However, that leads to the question as to where God gets his initial phase or primordial nature. He either gets it from Himself, in which case He is 'a Se,' or He gets it from another. If He gets it from Himself, then He is the exception to the general scope of Whitehead's metaphysics. Also, He is then being as such, and not becoming. If He gets it from another, He is not God, and we fall into an infinite regress, ultimately leading to God a Se, God as Pure Being, God as Pure Act.

The above is speculative. Viewing self-causation in the light of experience, we can note some defects there. It is true that we act for self-perfection and it is true that the lower grades of entities act for self-perfection. Still, we act for self-perfection through efficiency. Self-perfection attracts. Efficiency supplies the activity to attain the end. Also, we perfect other things through efficiency. We are the ones who turn stones into statues by our activity, by our ideas. It is not the block of marble that takes advantage of our activity to turn itself into a statue. The perfection of the block of marble becoming a statue, from the point of view of the marble, is a potency, which according to its act is a privation, and hence, in this respect, a negative thing. As a potency, it cannot reduce itself to act. We are the ones who educe the new form of a statue out of the marble, not the marble shaping itself. Even if Whitehead says that the finality of the block of marble is precisely to be marble, and not a statue, we can say that that is brought about not primarily by the components, but by the activity that combines calcium and carbon under certain conditions to be marble. If it be claimed that it is the natural tendancies in calcium and carbon to unite into marble, put into these as the initial phase of marble, we can still offer the rejoinder that in the long run, it is the activity that brings together what would not be brought together unless there were external activity to do so. Hence we see that from the metaphysical notion of causality, as well as from experience and empirical science, the emphasis in finality is attraction and not activity. We agree with Whitehead when he speaks of natural tendancies, but we disagree with him when he makes these tendancies self-causation through active unrest and not the reduction of these potencies through external activity.

2. *Efficient Cause*. When Whitehead describes efficient causality

as 'other formation' we agree. When he claims that it is causality by action, we agree. However, Whitehead apparently postulates that a thing becomes an efficient cause only when it has finished its stage of final cause, which would lead us to believe that an efficient cause acts without acting towards an end and acts when it has become a potency. Still, there is a lot in common between the Thomistic notion of efficient cause and Whitehead's notion of the same. Our disagreement is largely on the grounds that although according to him efficient cause works through activity, its activity is secondary to the activity of final cause. Furthermore, according to the Thomistic notion, it is the efficient cause which educes form from the potencies of matter through its activity by reducing potency to act following the attraction of an end. It is the efficient cause that educes the form of a statue from the matter in the making of a statue. In the sensitive world, it is the activity of the earthworm, following the desire for a good that causes it to make its way through the ground. In the vegetative world, it is the activity of the plant, following the desire for sunlight, that causes the stem to grow upwards, instead of downwards. In the inorganic world, it is the energy of heat together with the natural tendencies for molecular stability on the part of iron and sulphur that causes the two to unite into ferric sulphide. In all this, it is the activity of efficient cause that brings about the union of matter and form. The primary active cause is efficiency. With Whitehead, the primary active cause is finality, not efficiency.

3. *Formal Cause.* With Whitehead, a great many of the characteristics of our notion of formal cause are assumed by final cause. In Thomistic philosophy, it is form that determines a thing into a determined grade of being. In Whitehead's philosophy, that is done by the eternal object wherein the actual entity receives its initial phase. In Thomistic causality, one of the secondary activities of formal cause is to be the principle of activity in a being. Final cause, as the principle of unrest, has that function in the causality of Whitehead. According to Whitehead, formality is a mode of activity following the determination of the final cause. Formal cause keeps a being what it is by preventing it from uniting with the wrong entities. A being is made what it is by extrinsic form, which we have seen to be a contradiction. In that, Whitehead differs greatly from Thomistic formality. Of course, that is a logical consequence from the denial of substance as we under-

stand it. Where we have beings with a certain measure of stability, we have something intrinsic that determines it to be what it is. Where Whitehead has only concrescent actual entities, we would expect formality to be what it is, a mode of activity, the only thing in a concrescent entity that is permanent. What Whitehead overlooks is that this mode of permanence must have a permanent principle to make it what it is.

4. *Material Cause.* As we have seen before, Whitehead postulates only a quasi-material cause. Even this, though, shows that by the very fact that a thing can be a potential for other becomings, that it can be receptive of the action of other entities, necessitates in it an intrinsic principle of receptivity, an intrinsic principle that is not active. In other words, even admitting a quasi-material cause implicitly necessitates the denial of monism.

In conclusion, we might say that Whitehead does have a clear notion of causality. In many ways, especially where he treats of final cause as self-perfection, and where he treats of efficient cause as causation of other things by activity, he comes close to the Thomistic notion of causality. He differs where he speaks of final cause being self-causation, where he speaks of it as an active cause. He also differs where he treats of efficiency as a secondary form of action. He differs furthermore when he postulates extrinsic forms.

The presence of a theory of causality in a monistic philosophy is another example of the inconsistency of monism, with itself and with experience. In monism, in its principles, there can be no provision for differentiation into 'otherness,' no causality. Yet experience demands such a provision. Either theory or practice must be faced. Or else, either principles or experience must be sacrificed. Truth suffers from either choice *if* principles are averse to experience. Thomism easily reconciles them and guarantees the unity of Truth. Every monistic philosophy tries to reconcile them, but because principles are at odds with reality, monism must either sceptically proclaim experience an illusion, or attempt to erect a clumsy, weak, scarcely dependent system of reconciliation. The basic inconsistency in Whitehead's philosophy is this: if, as Whitehead claims, the actual entity is its own sufficient reason, it has no need of a cause. Yet Whitehead postulates a philosophy of cause. Hence, his philosophy is inconsistent.

SUMMARY

	Whitehead	St. Thomas
Nature of cause:	Reduction of self from potency to act; secondarily contribution of existence to another.	Contribution to the being or becoming of another with consequent dependence of effect upon cause.
Necessity of cause:	Not metaphysically required in a monistic philosophy, but cannot be ignored in view of experience. Hence fitted in.	Required on the part of composite beings insofar as such beings do not have the reason of their 'to be' in their essences.
Division and nature of each cause:		
(i) Material cause:	A potential for a new becoming.	That out of which something is made.
(ii) Formal cause:	Primarily an extrinsic principle of specification; secondarily a mode of action.	An intrinsic principle of specification; secondarily the source of qualities and operations.
(iii) Final cause:	An active principle of self-determination and self-causation.	That because of which a thing acts for the becoming; a principle of attraction, by reason of its appetibility, which attracts the efficient cause to action and which supposes the potency of a thing to tend to it. The cause of causes.
(iv) Efficient cause:	'other-causation' by action which is auxiliary to the action of the final cause.	Extrinsic, active principle which reduces the effect from potency to act.
Characteristics:	A system to explain the emergence of new entities; complicated and inconsistent because not required in a monistic philosophy. Does not give the sufficient reason for the becoming of new entities.	A simple and logical explanation of the reduction of something from potency to act; consistent with the entirety of Thomism. Thoroughly explains the sufficient reason of the beginning of new beings.

CHAPTER IX

Critique of Whitehead's Philosophy of God

For Thomistic philosophy, as well as for the philosophy of Whitehead, a treatise on the existence and nature of God is the ultimate and deepest application of metaphysics. Metaphysics treats of the ultimate causes of being itself, and God is the Ultimate Principle. The fundamental problem in metaphysics is that of the one and the many, and God is the Ultimate Explanation of that problem. Hence, any metaphysics is incomplete without a treatise on God.

We have seen that in Whitehead's philosophy God is more an example than a principle. He is the value phase, whereas the ultimate principle is process, or creativity. We have seen thus that although Whitehead has, implicit in his philosophy, proofs for the existence of God, these proofs do not arrive at God as Christianity knows Him. Whitehead's portrayal of God differs greatly from God as people worship Him.

Thomism has a much sounder approach to God, much sounder proofs for His existence, a much more solid explanation of His nature, and an equally tender appreciation of His omnipotent goodness and His infinite care for the world and its inhabitants.

Following Whitehead's scheme, we shall consider (i) the Christian concept of God; (ii) the proofs for God's existence; (iii) the Thomistic philosophical explanation for the Christian concept of the nature of God. In this, we shall follow St. Thomas Aquinas, who, metaphysician that he is, is at his philosophical best in treating of God.

As for the Christian concept of God, we can summarize it in the attributes of God. For the Christian, especially for the Christian philosopher, God is perfectly existing, insofar as His nature and His essence is to exist. Since He is perfect, He is without limitation (or potency), and hence Immutable, infinitely Good, Eternal, Omnipresent, infinitely knowing, infinitely loving (and thus, infinitely Tender), infinitely Just, infinitely Provident, infinitely Happy. God, having all these attributes, made the creatures that are the world and all beings in it in order that, analogically, they might participate in His being by imitation of Him according to their capacities; that rational or knowing creatures might, according to their capacities and their willingness, be happy by so imitating Him. We can find all these attributes—that is to say, the nature of God—preached in the Scriptures. However, here and now, this is a matter of philosophy and not of theology, and we limit ourselves to reason in investigating the existence and nature of God.

It is important to note that this comprehension of the nature of God exists in varying degrees not only among Christians but also among pagans, even if they are to be found in more or less garbled forms. This is a matter of anthropology, but the truth of this assertion is to be found in the folk-lore and arts of all peoples rather than in their philosophies. Thus, where Aristotle would make the First Immovable Mover an impersonal being, the Greek playwrights portray God or the gods as vitally personal beings. More pure notions of God may be found among more primitive peoples, which is the testimony—well-nigh universal testimony—of missionaries from all over the inhabited world. We might note here, that the existence of such notions of God require a sufficient reason.

Concerning the existence of God and the rational proofs advanced for God's existence, we can follow St. Thomas. His proofs, five in number, are thoroughly rational. Not once does he advance revelation as a proof. That does not show the superiority of reason over revelation, for revelation is the complement of reason (*not* its opponent), but it should be an incentive to non-Scholastic philosophers to give St. Thomas a hearing.

Starting from the fact that we can prove the existence of God not a priori (from principle to principiate, or from cause to effect), since we do not know God's nature yet, but a posteriori (from effect to cause), St. Thomas gives five proofs which are not limited to the scientist or to the philosopher, but which are based upon that knowledge which every man has, whereby he guides his life. St. Thomas's reasoning, with which Whitehead agrees, since he treats of the nature of God as indicated by the known world, is that from the knowledge of the nature of effects we can arrive at a certain knowledge of the nature of the cause.[1] To deny that is to exist in a world of scepticism and ultimately of solipsism. Instead

---

[1] *S.T.* I, 2, 1; I, 2, 2; cf. *C.G.* I, 10 & 11; I, 12, 14, 15.

of guaranteeing reason, it denies reason, and should logically conclude in taking faith as the only valid means of knowing.

St. Thomas's proofs are basically metaphysical.[2] They are a fivefold application of the principles of identity and sufficient reason. Again, they are based upon the knowability of things in themselves and the power of the mind to know the natures of things. Furthermore, they are an application of the Thomistic notion of potency and act to existing things. They answer the questions, "What are these things?" and "What is the explanation of things?" They are a five-fold answer to those two questions.

We can list the five proofs as follows:

1. From motion in the world to God the Unmoved Mover;
2. From created efficient causality to God the Uncaused Cause;
3. From contingency to God the absolutely Necessary Being;
4. From gradation of beings according to participation in being to God the Absolute Being;
5. From order in the world to God the Absolute Designer.

FIRST ARGUMENT: THE UNMOVED MOVER AS THE SUFFICIENT REASON FOR MOTION

St. Thomas bases this proof on the obvious existence of motion and change. Then he defines motion as the transition from potency to act, and says that in itself it is imperfect act. Now, we have seen that nothing can reduce itself from potency to act. It must be so reduced by something in act. Hence, motion or change is not a sufficient explanation of itself. It is explained only through dependence upon act. Act is the explanation of change.

Applying these principles to the world, we see a vast, closely united dependence of moving things upon movers. The movers are, to a certain extent, the explanation of the movement. But are they the complete explanation? We can say, with metaphysical certainty, that as long as a thing is moved (even though it be a mover) it is not a complete explanation of itself. As a mover it may explain other things, but as being moved it does not explain itself. For that, it depends upon something else. Hence, a series of moved movers, in itself, is no explanation of movement, motion, or change. The very fact that a mover is moved prevents its

---

[2] The following proofs are taken from *S.T.* P.Ia, Q. 2, A. 3, and from *C.G.* L. I, C. 13.

being the sufficient explanation of movement. Hence, the only sufficient explanation of motion is in the unmoved mover, put in motion by no other; "and this everyone understands to be God."

There is a common misunderstanding about this proof among writers in Catholic apologetics that a series is required for the validity of this proof. That is not the case. All that is needed is movement and the principle of sufficient reason. It is not the case of Object A being moved by Object B, and that by Object C, and so on down the line until we come to Object Z which is directly moved by God, Whose movement is passed on to Object Z, back through Y and X down to C, B, and A. It is not the case of moving a successive series of billiard balls or falling dominoes. With a proper understanding of potency and act, it is a case of showing that only one moved object cannot receive its sufficient reason in a mover which is moved, but in an unmoved mover containing therein no potency. As a matter of fact, there are any number of series of moved movers, but as a matter of principle they are not required. The movement in a moved thing is not explained, nor is it explained in a moved mover, for the being moved in a moved mover is not explained. The only explanation—direct as well as ultimate—in any moved object (whether it also be a mover) is God, the Unmoved Mover, Who is, by the very fact that He is unmoved, Pure Act.

THE SECOND ARGUMENT: THE UNCAUSED CAUSE THE SUFFICIENT REASON OF CAUSALITY

This argument is based upon the nature of efficient causes. As a prerequisite for it we must understand what we have seen in the last chapter that nothing can cause itself, for it would have to reduce itself from potency to act and would thus have to preexist itself. Hence for anything created to exist, it must be the effect of the action of something which preexists and causes it.[3]

Let us apply the principle of sufficient reason to the nature of cause and the nature of effect. Every effect requires a cause as its explanation, as its reason for existence. But what is its sufficient reason, its total explanation? It cannot be a caused cause, for such a cause is itself, from another point of view, an effect, and in turn requires a cause. Nor can a series of causes be the sufficient reason

---

[3] On the necessity of cause, see *De Ente et Essentia*, C. V; cf. *S.T.* P.Ia, Q. 3, A. 7; P.Ia, Q. 44, A. 1; *C.G.* L II, C. 15.

for cause and effect, for in a series of causes, each cause, by the fact that it is in a series, is thus an effect and hence not a sufficient explanation of itself. There must be an uncaused cause that pre-exists every other cause, and this is the Uncaused Cause "to which everyone gives the name God."

We may note that in this argument, also, a series of causes is not necessary for validity. There is a series of causes. There is secondary causality. However, the validity of the argument is simply this: any effect proves the existence of God, because any effect requires an uncaused cause as its sufficient reason. God is the Uncaused Cause. Therefore, any effect proves the existence of God. In explanation of that we may say, we must say, that an effect depends upon the Uncaused Cause either directly or indirectly; directly if immediately caused by God; indirectly if through other causes, which, for their validity as secondary causes depend by their nature upon the Uncaused Cause. Hence, any effect depends essentially upon the Uncaused Cause either immediately or mediately, and any effect has no meaning, no sufficient explanation, without the Uncaused Cause. The same is true for secondary causes, for they are effects.

THIRD ARGUMENT: THE ABSOLUTELY NECESSARY BEING AS THE SUFFICIENT REASON FOR CONTINGENT BEINGS

We start off this proof by considering the nature of contingent beings. A contingent being is that which has the possibility of not-being, or more simply, that which can not-be. A necessary being absolutely is that which in no way can not-be. A necessary being relatively is that which from a certain point of view and granted a given hypothesis cannot not-be. However, the relatively necessary being, in the last analysis, is contingent, for its necessity depends upon the postulation of an hypothesis.

Now, a contingent being, since it can not-be, is a limited being, restricted and limited by potency. Since it can not-be, it is not simply existence, but partakes of existence. In other words, every contingent being is an actualized possibility. Every contingent being is a being whose actual existence depends upon another. As the Thomist would say, "Omne ens contingens est ens ab alio," for nothing can reduce itself from possibility into actuality. It must be so reduced by something else already in act. If there were no principle to bring the possible into actual existence, it would not exist. Hence everything that has come to be has been brought into being by another, for every such creature is a composite of potency and act, which is to say that every creature that exists, has ever existed, or shall exist, is contingent, and hence, intrinsically dependent upon another for its existence.

Now, contingent beings can bring contingent beings into existence. Parents are contingent beings, and they bring children into existence. The same is true throughout all of creation. Hence, contingent beings can be partly explained by other contingent beings. However, that is not a sufficient explanation. The principle of sufficient reason is not satisfied by explaining 'entia ab alio' by 'entia ab alio.' The very fact that the producer is itself contingent proves the need for a sufficient reason for its own existence. The weak point in any producer is not going to be its productive action. That is its strong point, and partial explanation of production. The weak point in a producer is going to be its own production, the lack of explanation of its own production save in another producer. And since all production is not to be explained in a produced producer, it must be explained in an unproduced producer, an absolutely necessary being, a being who exists of himself, in his own right. Thus the very notion of existing by another necessitates the notion of a producer who exists of himself, "having of itself its own necessity, and not receiving it from another, but rather causing in others their necessity. "This all men speak of as God."

Does such a being exist? Yes. If he did not, there would be nothing. But there are many things whose contingency and whose necessity require a sufficient explanation. This explanation is to be found partly in their own necessity as producers, but their own being produced requires as a sufficient explanation an Unproduced Producer.

FOURTH ARGUMENT: THE ABSOLUTE BEING AS THE SUFFICIENT EXPLANATION OF GRADATION IN BEING

This proof is hailed by many Thomists as the deepest of the arguments for the existence of God. On the other hand, there are philosophers who either grant it only probable value, or who state that it is ontologism and no more.[4] The latter position can scarcely be held if this proof is viewed in the light of a fundamentally

---

[4] For example, Staab, Grunwald.

Thomistic principle, the analogy of being. However, let us investigate the argument to see if it itself clarifies whatever difficulties may be attached to it.

The fact is patent that few things are equal. Each individual, even though a member of a species or a genus, exists in a graded hierarchy of being according to its formal essence. As St. Thomas says, things are more or less noble, good, true, just as things are more or less hot. But gradation always supposes, as the sufficient reason of gradation, an absolute according to which things are graded. After all, before we can characterize gold alloys as 16, 18, or 20 karat gold, we must admit the objective existence of pure 24 karat gold. Objective gradation supposes an objective standard, or an objective absolute.

Similarly for being. Things exist as beings in gradation. A man has more being than a dog, a dog more than an insect. Furthermore, a man has a higher degree of being than an animal and a lesser degree than an angel. There is objective gradation of being. There are beings which exist in a state of 'more or less.' Hence, for a sufficient explanation of this gradation of being, there must be Absolute Being, just as before things can be more or less hot, heat must exist.

Is this ontologism? Is this supposing that our ideal of heat is objectified? I scarcely think so, if we understand St. Thomas correctly. To understand St. Thomas, we must understand how things are graded, and according to what principle they are graded. This is the doctrine of the analogy of being.

We have seen that a being is limited by its potencies, by its capacities. That makes the difference between saying that a thing *is* being and a thing *has*, or shares, being.[5] Each thing exists according to its own formal nature and differently than other things. A stone exists as an inorganic being, an animal as an organic being, a man as a rational being and a moral being. Thus, a man is good in a different way from an animal. An animal is good because it acts according to its nature, because it is what it is. A man has a special kind of goodness, moral goodness. Hence, a man has his existence and his being differently from other beings. Now, a man has this much in common with all things, including God, namely that he is. But he differs from other beings, including

---

[5] Cfr. *De Ente et Essentia*, C. V; *S.T.* P.Ia, Q. 44, A. 1.

God, that he has his own mode of existence. Hence, there is likeness and diversity in every thing that exists. The likeness is existence; the diversity is found in the manner in which the nature of the thing shares or participates in existence. Hence things exist, but things exist in different and diverse modes. In other words, existence is analogical and not univocal. If being were univocal, we would have to say that each thing is existence. But that would, logically, be the equivalent of saying that each thing exhausts existence, which would be the same as saying that each thing is absolute being, that all things are identical, that there is no differentiation. Such a proposition is absurd. Instead, we must say that each thing participates in or shares existence according to its natural capacities. Thus, the nature of a thing in reference to existence is that of potency to act.

We may thus say that there is gradation in being because there is participation in being according to higher or lower natures. And we must remember that the participation is *analogous*, not univocal. Now, obviously, that in which things participate must exist. We cannot participate objectively in an ideal. Extra-mental realities cannot participate in a mental being. Hence the being in which they participate must really and objectively exist.

Must this being in which all things participate be absolute? Again we must answer in the affirmative. That in which all things participate must have all the perfections of the things participating in it. It must be virtually all things. It must be the measure of all things. Can it be imperfect? No, for if it is imperfect, then it itself is limited, and it itself must participate thereby in a higher being. If the higher being is imperfect, not absolute, then it itself must participate in a still higher being, and so on until we come to absolute being in which all things participate, but participate analogously. In other words, the reason for gradation is the analogous participation of all things in absolute being, and only absolute being is the sufficient reason for beings which analogically participate in it.

Since this absolute being is the sufficient reason for all participation and all gradation, it must be the cause of it. Limited being has the explanation for its becoming and being in the absolute being, and hence the exemplary cause (as the measure of the natures of all things) as well as the efficient cause (as the sufficient reason for all things). "Therefore there must also be something which is to all beings as the cause of their being, goodness, and every other perfection; and this we call God."

Briefly, this is not pantheism. If the participation were univocal, as Spinoza would have it, it would be pantheism. Participation, however, is analogous, based upon the limitation of the individual participating natures according to potency. The great difference between God and His creatures is that He has within His nature no passive potency, whereas creatures are limited by potency.

FIFTH ARGUMENT: ABSOLUTE INTELLIGENCE AS THE SUFFICIENT REASON FOR ORDER IN THE UNIVERSE

This, I think, is the most patent of all the arguments for the existence of God. We may present it, briefly, thus: universal order necessitates the existence of a universal designing intelligence. There is universal cosmic order. Therefore, there is necessitated a Universal Designing Intelligence as the sufficient reason for this order, by which all things are directed towards their end. "This being we call God."

The fact of cosmic order exists. It is obvious in every entity that exists, among all entities, from the order of the ameba to the order of the planets, stars, nebulae. No one in his right mind can deny the necessity for intelligence in all of this and responsible for all this.

Must this intelligence be absolute? Yes, for if it were not, there would be no sufficient explanation for its ordered and orderly intelligence whereby it governs the universe.

Having gone through the Thomistic proofs for the existence of God, we may note the following points before considering the attributes and nature of God and before undertaking a critique of Whitehead's explanation of the existence and nature of God.

These proofs do not need a plurality of beings to arrive at the existence of God. As long as only one thing exists, we can reason our way to the existence of God. Anything that exists is what it is. As a composite of act and potency it is changing, caused, contingent, measured in its participation in existence, designed and part of a great design. Each and all of these attributes of it and its nature demand God the Fulness of Being, the Uncaused Cause, the Unmoved Mover, the absolutely Necessary Being, the Absolute Designing Intelligence, as its sufficient reason.

Secondly, we may note that the five proofs for God's existence preclude any notion of things except God existing in complete independence. Things have a certain measure of subsistence, true, but the entire universe is a system of contingent and interdependent beings, each depending upon the other, and all depending upon God as their sufficient explanation. Hence, Thomism is much more complete in its explanation of the 'organic universe' than Whitehead, save that it disagrees with Whitehead in projecting biological organism into non-organic existence, and proclaims that physical organization is not a sufficient explanation of life.

THE NATURE AND ATTRIBUTES OF GOD

We arrive at the nature and attributes of God by negation and attribution of analogy. Thus it is that St. Augustine says that it is easier to know what God is not than to know what He is. He is not denying that we can know anything positive about God, but he is affirming that we arrive at those positive notes by denying in God the limitations of creatures. St. Thomas does the same, follows the same procedure, and arrives at the positive nature and positive attributes of God by denying Him the limitations of creatures. This we have seen in the proofs for the existence of God. We deny in God transition from potency to act, His being caused, His being contingent, His participating in anything, His being designed, and thus at the same time we affirm of Him that He is Pure Act (the Unmoved Mover), First (Uncaused) Cause, absolutely Necessary, absolutely Existing, and Absolute Intelligence. These positive notes are the roots of the attributes of God, and in themselves are manifestations of God Pure Act.

The basic attribute of God is that He is Pure Act. We have seen that act is synonymous with being, and that potency is a capacity and a limitation of being. If God is Pure Act, then He has no limitations. Hence He is the Fulness of Being and all perfections, the Measure of all things. God as the Measure of all things, which we have seen proved from the fourth proof, is important in reference to creation and providence. God sees and cares for every individual entity since He sees every entity as a graded imitation of Himself, and hence an analogical participation in His nature. God sees all things in Himself. We shall return to this point in considering Whitehead's rejection of the altogether abstract, self-contemplative deity of Aristotle.

God Pure Act is the basis and foundation of the absolute

attributes, namely those attributes which pertain to God's immanent life, and the relative attributes, which pertain to God's transcient action. (It is true that theologians speak of relative attributes in God's Immanent Life, those attributes among the Three Persons of the Trinity. This, however, is a question of theology. When it comes to the Trinity, philosophy merely shows the non-repugnance of the Trinity, which we know by revelation.)

The deepest thing we can say of God is that His Essence is His Existence.[6] There is no distinction between them. That is the full meaning of the text from Exodus: "I am Who am."[7] God's Essence is His Existence because He is Pure Act, and hence, Pure Existential Being. There is no limitation in Him, for passive potency is the principle of limitation. If there is no passive potency in Him, He cannot participate in being, for participation demands limitation. Hence, He *is* being, univocally, and therefore the Fulness of Being, of Whom all other being is an imitation.

Because He is Pure Act, He is the fulness of all perfections.[8] As Pure Act and the Fulness of Being, He is unlimited in regard to time and space, and hence is Eternal (without beginning or end) and everywhere. He is Eternal, especially, because as Pure Act He has no principle of corruption, and hence, cannot end. Nor can He begin, because a beginning, as a transition from potency to act, presupposes potency, which is not in God. As Pure Act, He can in no way be a composition. Thus in His Essence, He is Immutable and absolutely Simple.

As Pure Act, He has no limitations, hence He is Infinite. He has all known perfections, either formally or virtually (as a cause),[9] in an infinite manner. Thus, He is all knowing, all loving, all just. These latter three are also relative attributes, and serve as a transition to the relative attributes.

The relative attributes suppose creation. By creation we mean the producing of things where nothing was. Every contingent thing must come into being. Hence there must be creation. What is the Christian philosophy of creation? It is to be found in God's Infinite Goodness and Infinite Happiness. God, as Pure Act, is

---

[6] *S.T.* P.Ia, Q. 3, A. 2, 3, & 4.
[7] *Exodus*, II, 14.
[8] *S.T.* P.Ia, Q. 4, A. 1 & 2.
[9] *S.T.* P.Ia, q. 4, a. 2.

perfectly happy and Good in Himself. God's Being is imitable, as we have seen, analogically. God, from all eternity, knows all the ways in which His Being can be imitated. These modes of imitation are the possibles. God reduces some of them to actuality, and all things exist as imitations of God in a gradation of existence, which gradation is determined by the natures of individual things.

Because creatures are imitations of God, God knows all ways in which His Nature is imitated.[10] Hence He knows all things more intimately than they know themselves, for He is the Cause and Designer of them. Because He thus knows them and because they, as contingent beings, depend upon Him at every moment of their existence as upon their sufficient reason, He provides for them. This is His Providence[11] His continued creation. Hence, Aristotle was wrong in saying that God had no care for the world. Aristotle failed to understand that God sees, knows, and cares for all things, because Aristotle failed to see that God knows all things *in Himself*, as imitations of His Being.

Since all things are imitations of God, they are good.[12] Since they are good, God, in loving their goodness, loves them. Hence, His Providence and His Love for things show Him to be infinitely tender and merciful. Moral evil does not come from God. Although, because of the gradation and corruption of creatures, and because some creatures fail to reach their end, God may be said to be the accidental cause of physical evil, still, He is not the cause of moral evil.[13] Moral evil comes from voluntary deordination, which flows from man's free will. Hence, God is the Author of good; man the author of moral evil. Because there is a choice between good and evil, there is a right and a wrong way of operation on the part of creatures. Hence there is law. Because God, the Measure of all things and the Ultimate Source of all law, demands good, and hence right operation, God is infinitely Just.[14] Because God desires the right done, and because as Infinite Goodness He respects the sincerity of the repentent sinner, He is infinitely forgiving. He is not "a little oblivious as to morals." He is forgiving as to sin, as long as the sinner is sincerely contrite.

---

[10] *S.T.* P.Ia, Q. 14, A. 11.
[11] *S.T.* P.Ia, Q. 22, A. 1–4.
[12] *S.T.* P.Ia, Q. 6, A. 4; cfr. P.Ia, Q. 21, A. 4.
[13] *S.T.* P.Ia, Q. 49, A. 2.
[14] *S.T.* P.Ia, Q. 21, A. 2.

The above is only a sketch, so to speak, of the attributes and nature of God. Yet it is sufficient, I think, to point out the utter logical cohesiveness of the Christian philosophy of God. The proofs for the existence of God, metaphysically sound, give us the basic foundation of God as Pure Act. That is the foundation upon which we build our understanding of the infinitely Good and Loving God of Christian revelation. It also gives us a starting point for our critique of Whitehead's understanding of God.

Critique of Whitehead's Philosophy of God

It is obvious that Whitehead's notion of God differs widely from the Christian and traditional notion. Whitehead's basic criticism of the Christian notion is, due to Aristotelianism, the making of a Caesar out of God, thus combining the Jewish notion of God as power with the Greek notion of God as subsistent wisdom. Since God was made a Caesar, the Christian revelation of Love was overlooked. Whitehead seems to hold that Aristotle dictated Christian doctrine.

I wonder how anyone in any way familiar with Church history, especially with patrology, could hold that position. Any study of Christian antiquities brings out the emphasis of God as Love. Any study of the Patristic writings shows clearly that the Fathers of the Church had no difficulty reconciling their philosophical explanations of God—whether Platonic or Aristotelian—with the doctrine that God is Love. That is because reason and revelation complement each other. Revelation complements reason, and brings to reason truths beyond the scope of reason or difficult of attainment on the part of reason. Reason, on the other hand, expands and applies the truths of revelation. The great thinkers have been those who have put reason to work, not only in its own proper sphere, but also in the service of Faith, by at least proving the non-contradiction of mysteries of Faith.

Whitehead has a point in that Christians do not adore the God of Christian philosophy. They adore the God of Christian revelation. Philosophy can prove the existence of God, and something of the attributes of God. However, in its own right, it cannot undertake the question of the Persons in God, and we adore a person, not a nature. Christians do not say prayers in honor of the First Immovable Mover, the Uncaused Cause, the absolutely

Necessary Being. They pray to God the Father, God the Son, God the Holy Ghost.

However, where Whitehead would distinguish between the two, namely, between a personal God and the God of metaphysics by making the former subordinate to the ultimate principle of process, and by denying the latter, Christianity has affirmed and proved, through the great minds of the Church, as well as in the philosophies of Plato, Aristotle, and the Platonists and Aristotelians, that the two are the same. Let us use this as the basis of our critique of Whitehead's theodicy, namely, a critique of the metaphysical values involved in Whitehead's notion of God as the 'value phase.'

We have seen earlier in this chapter that we can start with the same premises that are held by Whitehead and arrive at the existence and attributes of the God of Christian revelation. We can do that because we have seen that to say that change is the ultimate reality is not to give the sufficient reason of change. We have seen that change means changing things, that an entity must be an existing being before it can operate, that to say that the essence of anything is becoming is to affirm a contradiction. Once we grant that change means changing things, or things passing from potency to act, we must affirm that change is as wide as created reality. We must admit that the created universe is a vast interorganization of contingency and dependency, and that from the interorganization we must arrive at God as the Fulness of Being, the absolutely Necessary Being, Whose essence is absolutely perfect existence. We must thus arrive at God for the completely sufficient explanation of any and every thing. It is only when we have God as portrayed by Thomistic philosophy as the ultimate explanation of everything that we can say, in Whitehead's own words, that:

> "Speculative philosophy is the endeavour to frame a coherent, logical, necessary system of general ideas in terms of which every element of our experience can be interpreted."[15]

It is only in the Thomistic explanation of God that we find the ultimate answer to the basic philosophical problem of the One and the Many. That answer is to be found only in Being which *is*

---

[15] *Process and Reality*, p. 2.

existence (God) and being which *has* existence; in Being which is Pure Act and being which is a composition of potency and act.

That much we have seen in the Thomistic proofs for the existence of God, based as they are on the nature of any created thing. Yet, as a philosopher of becoming, Whitehead, has professedly repudiated such reasoning, sound as it may be. We must admit that outside of the Thomistic school of philosophy (with rare exceptions) and even within the Scholastic school, St. Thomas is ignored. Let us, then, once again turn to Whitehead's own position, especially his postulate of God as the 'value phase' and see if we cannot, by applying Thomistic principles, turn Whitehead's arguments in favor of the Thomistic notion of God.

It is from the twofold fact of activity and permanence that we arise to the notion of God. We do this through the notion of potency (the determinable principle) and act (the determining principle) as well as through the analogy of being, or participation in being. We must note that potency and act and participation in being are notions which are accepted by Whitehead. In this development, we shall argue from the notion of value in relation to potency and act.

Potency, as we have seen, is twofold. Passive potency may be defined as a 'real capacity for the reception of perfection.' Whitehead would call it a being in 'objective immortality.' Active potency is 'a principle of operation.' That is fundamental in Whitehead's 'prehensions.' Act is a perfection towards which potency tends.

Now, let us substitute for 'perfection' the notion of 'value.' A perfection is a value, and I think that Whitehead would agree to this substitution. Thus, we can define potency as a 'real capacity for the reception of value,' which is in sound agreement with the entire philosophy of Whitehead. He has to hold that if he desires to retain his cosmic, organic evolution.

To continue the argument: the world is full of individual things evolving, that is, tending towards value. The reception of value is limited by the capacities of each thing to receive value, much as water is limited by the vessel which contains it. A plant cannot receive the value that an animal can receive, nor can a brute animal receive the value that a rational animal can.

These tendencies to value cannot explain themselves. Hence they must be explicable as formal participations in the value

Critique of Whitehead's Philosophy of God   161

towards which they tend. This is again fundamental in Whitehead's philosophy. Thus, the tendency of a plant towards its individual value is only explicable in terms of the value to be attained, just as formally every potency is measure and explained by the act towards which it tends. If a thing is attainable, it is a value for the thing tending to it. This is the philosophy of evolution. Everything is working to attain a better and higher state, to attain value, which value is the explanation of the tendencies towards that value. After all, if a thing participates in something, that something in which it participates must exist.

That is the explanation given by the philosophers of becoming, but does it go far enough? Whitehead makes God part of the process, and not the ultimate. But that shows some deficiency in God, for God must evolve, too. This is characteristic of Whitehead's postulates of the 'primordial' and 'consequent' natures of God. This is to say that God is lacking in and tending to value. This is also to say that He cannot be the highest value, since, by the very fact that He is evolving, tending, is to say that He lacks value. He is only, then, an intermediate value. To say that He is perfected by things being absorbed into Him does not give a sufficient reason, for because these things tend to God, He is a higher value than they are, and He cannot be satisfied with values lower than Himself.

Suppose, then, that the value towards which He tends is process. It, too, is insufficient, for it too is tending towards something higher and hence is insufficient. If God is in process, He is imperfect, even though He does perfect Himself somewhat by absorbing things into His nature. If He tends towards process, He is imperfect, for He is, at any event, lacking some perfection (value) by the fact that He is tending. Process itself is lacking in value by the fact that it is tending to a higher state, and hence is not a sufficient explanation of itself. To explain a tendency by a tendency is to fall into the old fallacy of explaining things 'idem per idem.'

Process, then, does not explain itself. It cannot be the ultimate. It does not explain God, for God tends to process which cannot explain itself. God does not explain Himself, and hence cannot explain the quest for value on the part of lower entities. It amounts to this, that the only explanation for the universal—cosmic as well as individual—quest for value is to be found in Value itself, in that which *is* value and does not share in it, in that which has no process in its nature, for process implies imperfection and a tendency towards perfection, and that which contains imperfection cannot be said to be a sufficient explanation of itself. Thus, participation in value, by its very nature, requires the objective existence of value in which there is no imperfection. But such a fulness of value cannot have within it any potency, cannot be limited in any way, for it then would be tending towards a higher value, and would not be a sufficient explanation of itself, but would have to depend, for its explanation, on that which has no imperfection within it. Hence this value must be Pure Act, Fulness of Being, the explanation for all tendencies to value, and, to quote St. Thomas, ". . . this we call God."[16]

Nor can it be objected, on metaphysical grounds, that God as Pure Act is an absentee landlord, the ruthless Caesar, the image of the Oriental despot. By the very fact that value tends to fulfillment in Him, by the fact that He is responsible—and thus the cause—for value in entities means that He either forgets them (which is impossible if He is Pure Act), or He thinks of them (to speak anthropomorphically). In seeing them, He sees them as formal imitations and participations of and in Himself, and hence He loves them as imitations of Himself. Thus He has a much closer and much more tender care for the world than Whitehead's vague recompense for cosmic disorder. The Christian God is much more personal than the cosmic God or value phase.

The Thomist will recognize in all above the fourth proof of St. Thomas for the existence of God as the summary of the first four proofs. He will also recognize the basis for the Thomistic real distinction between essence and existence, as well as the basis for St. Thomas's explanation of the attributes of God. We can see here where the philosophy of St. Thomas is always a sound refutation against some of the anthropomorphic theodicies of contemporaries who would attempt to explain all in terms of a particular science. We can also see the force of the identity of good with being. We have seen how value must be synonymous with being to have any meaning, and we can thus see the living quality of the transcendentals as well as the timeless and ever available value of Thomistic metaphysics.

---

[16] *S.T.* P.Ia, Q. 2, A. 3, at the end of each proof for God's existence.

But far beyond this, and as the complement to all this, we must see the true role of philosophy in relation to revelation. Natural knowledge, profound and deep as it may be, is incomplete. The fact that Whitehead has spent many years in deep thinking—hampered by his background, yes, but nevertheless deep thinking—and has arrived at a notion of God that fails to satisfy man's naturally inquisitive mind, is another example of what St. Thomas teaches in the *Summa Contra Gentiles*[17] that for a true knowledge of God (and hence of anything) we need revelation, the complement to our knowledge, the guide and guardian of our thinking.

SUMMARY

	Whitehead	St. Thomas
Necessity of God:	As the guiding reason and value phase of each individual entity. To guarantee individual, social, and cosmic order; to avoid frustration in entities and to draw good out of evil.	As the ultimate sufficient reason of each and every thing that ever was, is, and shall be—The First Efficient and Ultimate Final Cause of the Universe.
Nature of God:	The highest example of the actual entity, eternally undergoing the process of guiding and assigning value to the lesser events that are the world; constantly enriching himself. The locus of the eternal objects.	Pure Act, absolutely Necessary Being; the Fulness of Being without limitation or change.
Attributes of God:	Eternal change subject to creativity in his: (i) primordial nature—the ideal, the urge of attainment on the part of lesser actual entities. (ii) consequent nature—the fulfillment of satisfaction of lower entities in God, the enrichment of God by his gaining of actuality in lower entities.	Application of God Pure Act. (i) Absolute attributes Infinite Eternal Immutable Absolute Unity, Truth, Goodness (ii) Relative Attributes Creator, Conserver Concurrer Provident All Loving All Just

---

[17] *C.G.*, L. I, c. 4.

	(iii) superjective nature—the reassigning of new values to new entities. This is the 'kingdom of heaven,' the saving of what might have been lost.	Source of all law and authority.
Proofs for existence:	Contingency Gradation of entities Cosmic order Memory Finality	Motion Efficient Cause Contingency Gradation of beings (formality) Design (finality)
Characteristics:	An unsound and incomplete philosophy of God which can but fails to prove the existence and nature of God. In making God subordinate to creativity, it deprives Whitehead's entire philosophy of a sufficient reason.	The simple and logical ultimate in a metaphysically sound philosophy.
		The ultimate answer and sufficient reason of every thing and every problem.
	Each proof incomplete and more a postulate than a proof.	Each proof the application of the principle of sufficient reason.

GENERAL CONCLUSION

We have seen Whitehead's philosophical aim, namely, to formulate a system of general, coherent, and logical principles to explain each and every item of experience. We have seen the system that he has erected in order to attain that aim. What, now, is our general conclusion?

We may say, with all respect, that despite his careful efforts, he fails to attain his proposed object. All the way through his philosophy, from his theory of knowledge, in the actual entity and in every application of the actual entity in (i) its nature, (ii) its role in causality, (iii) in its exemplification in the nature of God,—in all these he leaves many problems unsolved. Hence, he does not explain every item of experience. In fact, his basic principles rather lead away from experience in such a way that he is forced to postulate a complex and somewhat ungainly philosophical structure in an attempt to cover the weaknesses of his philosophy.

What, may we say, is the basic weakness in his philosophy? I think we must answer that it is in his approach to reality. We have seen that his theory of knowledge is empirical and mathematical. Empiricism fails to show objective principles in extramental reality and is an implicit denial of the power of the intellect to know reality from its own proper object, that is, the being of things. Further, while mathematical abstraction supposes a power of the intellect to consider the sense data, the specific sense data of quantity, by its very nature it tends to abstract from a deeper appreciation of reality as such. Hence, it views reality in terms of mathematical relations, and projects relativism into reality while overlooking the fundamental principle that relation supposes substance.

Because his degree of abstraction is not sufficiently deep, Whitehead's understanding and application of the principles of identity, non-contradiction, and sufficient reason correspondingly lack an appropriate depth. He maintains these principles, for they are implicit in his philosophy, but he does not follow them far enough.

Thus he fails to realize that:

1. The nature of the actual entity, which as we have seen reduces itself to subsistent becoming, must either lead to substance or resolve itself into a contradiction. Thus it can be the sufficient reason neither of itself nor of reality.

2. Relation must either lead to substance or remain an ideal.

3. Causality must either lead to substance or else have no meaning.

4. God must be Pure Act, not only immanent in but also infinitely transcendent to the world in order to be the sufficient reason of anything or in order that the sufficient reason of anything be known.

Briefly, then, we may say that Whitehead's dynamic, relativistic, monism fails because his comprehension of potency and act is incomplete. Does that mean that Whitehead is a superficial thinker? I do not think so. The mental acumen and sincerity of thought that are his have been diverted and diffused because of his background.

The mention of his background brings to mind one last thought. What are our qualifications to criticize the philosophy of a man who has spent so many years in careful and systematic thought? Our standard of criticism is our own philosophical heritage, the ever-deep, ever-living, eminently real philosophy, the philosophical tradition which receives its fullest expression in St. Thomas.

Whitehead has sincerely worked for many years on his philosophical heritage, but what a satisfying difference is there in the philosophy of St. Thomas! What a far deeper, far more simple, for more certain explanation we find! Starting from the nature of the human mind to know and understand the nature of being and beings, we study them through their accidents to their essence. In this study, we find:

1. The intrinsic nature of substances, composed as they are of potency and act. Whence we are led to the sufficient reason of their:

2. Becoming, being, and passing away. As a sufficient reason of this, we pass to

3. Causality, which is the sufficient explanation of all things which do not have their existence identical with their essence. Causality, and the contingency of beings through participation demand, as their sufficient reason:

4. God, Pure Act, the Fulness of Being, in Whom is no limitation, Who is the ultimate sufficient reason of Himself and of every being, actual and possible.

Whether or not St. Thomas knew it, he wrote one of the shortest autobiographies known to man, when in the first chapter of the first book of the *Summa Contra Gentiles* he wrote his spirit and his life in the words of another great philosopher:

"Sapientis est causas altissimas considerare."

BIBLIOGRAPHY

Sources

Aquinas, T. *Summa Theologica.* Leonine Edition. Ex Typographia Polyglotta S.C. de Propaganda Fidei, Rome, 1888.

——*Summa Contra Gentiles.* Same edition.

——*De Ente et Essentia.* Taken from *Sancti Thomae Aquinatis Opera,* Vol. IV. Lethielleux, Paris.

——*De Principiis Naturae ad Fratrem Sylvestrum.* Opusculum 27, Vives edition (31, Roman Edition). Vives, Paris, 1875. Vol. 27.

——*In Metaphysicam Aristotelis Commentarium.* Marietti, Turin, 1926.

——*Quaestiones Disputatae de Veritate.*

——*Quaestiones Disputatae de Potentia.*

——*Quaestiones Disputatae de Spiritualibus Creaturis.*

All from *Divi Thomae Opera,* Bettinelli, Venice, 1745-1760.

Aristotle. *Physics* (translation by Harold H. Joachim).

——*Metaphysics* (translation by W. D. Ross).

——*On Generation and Corruption* (translation by Harold H. Joachim).

All taken from *The Basic Works of Aristotle,* Richard McKeon, editor, University of Chicago. Random House, N. Y., 1941.

Augustine. *Confessions.*

——*The City of God.*

Both taken from the *Nicene and Post-Nicene Fathers,* Charles Scribner's Sons, N. Y., 1908.

Plato. *The Sophist.* Jowett Edition; Charles Scribner's Sons, N. Y., 1895.

——*Symposium.* Jowett Translation; Charles Scribner's Sons, N. Y., 1895.

——*Timaeus* (translation by Henry Davis, M.A.) from *The Works of Plato,* George Bell & Sons, London, 1900.

——*Thaetetus.* Jowett translation; Carlton House, N. Y., 1929.

Whitehead, A. N. *Process and Reality.* Macmillan & Co., N. Y., 1929.

——*Adventures of Ideas.* At the University Press, Cambridge, 1933.

——*Science and the Modern World.* Macmillan, N. Y., 1925.

——*The Concept of Nature.* At the University Press, Cambridge, 1920.

——*Modes of Thought.* Macmillan, N. Y., 1938.

——*The Principle of Relativity.* At the University Press, Cambridge, 1922.

——*The Function of Reason.* Princeton University Press, New Jersey, 1929.

——*The Principles of Natural Knowledge.* At the University Press, Cambridge, 1925.

——*Religion in the Making.* Macmillan, N. Y., 1926.

——*Symbolism, Its Meaning and Effect.* At the University Press, Cambridge, 1925.

Secondary Sources:

Calkins, M. *The Persistent Problems of Philosophy.* Macmillan, N. Y., 1925,

Coffey, P. *Ontology.* Longmanns, Green, N. Y., 1929.

Garrigou-Lagrange, R. *God, His Existence and His Nature.* (Translated from the French by Dom Bede Rose, O.S.B., D.D.). Herder, St. Louis, 1934.

Gilson, E. *The Philosophy of St. Thomas Aquinas.* (Translated from the French by Edward Bullough, M.A.) Herder, St. Louis, 1939.

——*The Spirit of Medieval Philosophy* (translated from the French by A. H. C. Downes). Scribner's, N. Y., 1940.

Gonzalez, Z. *Histoire de la Philosophie.* (Translated from the Spanish by G. de Pascal). Lethielleux, Paris, 1891.

Gredt, J. *Elementa Philosophiae Aristotelico-Thomisticae.* Herder, Freiburg, 1932.

John of St. Thomas. *Cursus Philosophicus Thomisticus.* Marietti, Turin, 1933.

Hocking, W. E. *Science and the Idea of God.* The University of North Carolina Press, Chapel Hill, N. C., 1944.

Hugon, E. *Cursus Philosophiae Thomisticae.* Lethieulleux, Paris, 1934.

Joad, C. E. M. *Philosophical Aspects of Modern Science.* Macmillan, N. Y., 1933.

Keppler, T. *Contemporary Religious Thought.* (An anthology compiled by Thomas W. Keppler). Abingdon-Cokesbury Press, N. Y., 1941.

Maritain, J. *An Introduction to Philosophy.* Longmanns Green, N. Y., 1930.

——*A Preface to Metaphysics.* Sheed & Ward, N. Y., 1939.

Meehan, F. X. *Efficient Causality in Aristotle and St. Thomas.* Catholic University of America Press, Washington, D. C., 1940.

Renard, H. *The Philosophy of Being.* The Bruce Publishing Co., Milwaukee, Wis., 1943.

Sheen, Fulton J. *Philosophy of Science.* Bruce, Milwaukee, 1934.

Schilpp, P. A. *The Philosophy of Alfred North Whitehead.* (Edited by Paul Arthur Schilpp), from *The Library of Living Philosophers*, Vol. III; Northwestern University, Evanston and Chicago, 1941.

Ueberwegg. *A History of Philosophy.* Scribner's N. Y., 1871.

Watkin, E. I. *A Philosophy of Form.* Sheed & Ward, N. Y., 1935.

Wieman & Meland. *American Philosophies of Religion.* Willett, Clark & Co., Chicago, 1936.

Revues and Articles:

Lintz, Edward J. *The Unity in the Universe According to Alfred North Whitehead.* From *The Thomist;* Vol. VI, Number 2. July, 1943.

O'Brien, John A. *"God" in Whitehead's Philosophy.* From *The American Ecclesiastical Review;* Vol. CX, Number 6; June 1944. Vol. CXI, Number 2; August 1944.

O'Grady, Daniel C. *Mathematics and Philosophy.* From *The New Scholasticism;* Vol. VI, Number 2. April 1932.

Sheen, Fulton J. *Professor Whitehead and the Making of Religion.* From *The New Scholasticism;* Vol. I, Number 2, April 1927.

Schabert, J. A. *The Organic Realism of Whitehead.* Proceedings of the Eighth Annual Meeting of the American Catholic Philosophical Association, December 1932.

Whitehead, A. N. *Religion and Science. Atlantic Monthly,* Vol. 136, August 1925.

Note: For a complete, contemporary, non-Scholastic view of Whitehead's philosophy, the book *The Philosophy of Alfred North Whitehead*, edited by

Paul Arthur Schilpp and listed above in this bibliography, is particularly valuable. This work is a symposium of eighteen articles contributed by eighteen non-Scholastic philosophers which adequately covers every phase of Whitehead's system as it is considered by contemporary non-Scholastic philosophers. It also serves as a valuable indication of the non-Scholastic mind concerning philosophy in general. For the non-Scholastic view on Whitehead's philosophy, the following works (among many) are suggested:

Braham, E. G.   *The Place of God in A. N. Whitehead's Philosophy.* London Quarterly Reviaw, Vol. 164, pp. 63-69. Jan. 1939.
Cory, D.   *Dr. Whitehead on Perception.* Journal of Philosophy; Vol. 30, pp. 29-43. Jan. 19, 1933.
Murphy, A. E.   *Objective Relativism in Dewey and Whitehead.* Philosophical Review, Vol. 36; pp. 121-144. March 1944.
Taylor, A. E.   *Dr. Whitehead's Philosophy of ¦Religion.* Dublin Review, Vol. 181, pp. 17-41. July 1927.
Wieman.   *Professor Whitehead's Concept of God.* Hibbert Journal, Vol. 25, pp. 623-630.
Winn, R. B.   *Whitehead's Concept of Process, A Few Critical Remarks.* Journal of Philosophy, Vol. 30, pp. 710-714. Dec. 21, 1933.

www.ingramcontent.com/pod-product-compliance
Lightning Source LLC
Chambersburg PA
CBHW070923180426
43192CB00037B/1735